VENICE
The KEYS to the CITY
The ASTUTE TRAVELER'S Guide

PATTY CIVALLERI

D1557139

1-TAKE
MULTIMEDIA | PUBLICATIONS

COPYRIGHT

1-TAKE MultiMedia | Publishing
6216 Pacific Coast Hwy, Suite 321
Long Beach, CA 90803
www.1TAKE.com

Ordering Information:
Quantity sales. Special discounts are available for quantity purchases by corporations, associations, and others. For details, contact the publisher at the address above.
Orders by U.S., Canadian, and UK trade bookstores and wholesalers, please contact:
MidPoint Trade
27 West 20th Street, Suite 1102
New York, NY 10011
MidPointTrade.com

Printed in South Korea.

Publisher's Cataloging-in-Publication data Civalleri, Patty.
VENICE: A Traveler's Guide to Getting Lost / Patty Civalleri.
ISBN-10:0-9981926-5-1
ISBN-13:978-0-9981926-5-9

1. Travel.
2. Italy/Venice
3. European History.
4. Art History

First Edition
1 2 3 4 5 HPSK 22 21 20 19 18

To the man that instilled in me the love of writing and
made it so natural for me. This gift has served me well
throughout my life. Your love and support has kept me
propped up during those tough days.
I am glad you are so near, Dad. ♥

Acknowledgments

I am thankful to the **Italian National Tourist Board**
in Los Angeles who helped me to begin this project by
pointing me in the right direction and to the right people.
The MUVE Civic Museum Foundation of Venice was
tremendously helpful with gaining me access to people and places that would normally be shut off from a
typical visitor, and in a city where I was friendless, they
made me feel not so alone. Seba and Val from Venezia
Autentica were patient with my endless questions, and
were always ready with a good bottle of Prosecco. Sylvia
Zanella: author, Burano expert, and friend, thank you
for your kindness and "Cheers" to the success of your
own marvelous book! Roger, you are my biggest fan and
supporter: every time I take off on my wild dreams, you
are always there to push me just a little further ~ with so
much love to keep me company. Thank you for bolster-
ing my spirits when things appear glum.

An extra special thanks to **Tiziano Cini,** who has been
a welcome consultant. Only a Fire Chief can possess
the keen knowledge of every tiny corner of a city, and
you were so willing to share the secrets of your beloved
Venice with me. Most especially, I thank you for your
friendship.

La Serenissima

la ser-eh-NEE-see-ma

The Most Serene Republic of Venice

Originally bestowed by the Byzantines upon the Doge, this title was ultimately used to describe the entire Republic of Venice. As a land known for its wealth, comfort, fairness of attitude, and peace of mind, it maintained its reputation as a calm and peaceful destination. It seemed immune to the pitfalls of negative politics, poverty, and general discomfort. Citizens from Western Europe and the Middle East would dream of visiting Venice if their means would allow.

TABLE of CONTENTS

TABLE of CONTENTS

HOW TO USE THIS BOOK

Don't read this like an ordinary book. Find your own interests on page **13**. Thumb through it randomly, in any order that interests you.

When you find a little lock, pay attention to it; that's just me letting you know that I found a special or rare treat or surprise that is not commonly known by the masses, and I've unlocked this little secret just for you.

The little red numbers **12** simply refer to page numbers.

Yup, you guessed it! You have found a great place to enjoy a nice cold gelato. And I promise they won't be hard to find!

Venice thinks of themselves in terms of neighborhoods or "Sestieri." The color system used in this book follows this schema:

SAN MARCO	CASTELLO	CANNAREGIO
SAN POLO	DORSODURO	SANTA CROCE

QUEST BOX

If you're up to having a little fun, we have included some random things to find around the city. This is great for both kids and adults alike. Look for these YELLOW dotted boxes and enjoy discovering new things on your way to solving each quest.

The "...at a glance" pages will give you a brief glance at what is coming up in the section.

..at a glance

BUT not all "glances" will have a longer explanation. Some are simply tiny little finds that don't warrant a larger explanation, but we thought you might want to know about them anyway.

Did You Know...

Blue boxes will share trivia, factoids, stories, and tales. These are great for picking up fast facts about the place or area you are visiting, like the one below...

"The word 'Italy' is a geographic expression, a description which is useful to shorthand, but has no political significance." ~ in a letter from Austrian Statesman Klemens von Metternich c.1847

INTRODUCTION

WELCOME TO VENICE
You're not in Italy any more!

I came to Venice with no pre-conceived notions about the city; no template in which to conform to when writing this book. Instead, I wanted to simply roam her streets, meet her people, and use all of my senses to find the true heart of Venice. I wanted her to whisper her story and to share her innermost secrets with me.

Week after week, I wandered her streets, museums, restaurants, and shops, waiting to hear her faint whispers.

After a couple of months, I realized that she had been whispering to me all along; I simply needed to listen. So, I did.

She spoke of a vast 1500-year history of anguish and angst; of scores of people who fled their mainland homes and communities to be safe from barbarians like Attila the Hun; who struggled to build a safe haven upon the soft and marshy swamplands; who stood tall to create a stabilized Republic as a new backbone of strength and safety; of a military might to protect as well as to conquer and grow; of a system of Capitalism to ensure that her residents were fed and fulfilled; of a structure of trade so powerful that it opened up new paths of products, cultures, and philosophies into the Western World.

Her beauty and power shown like a gleaming gemstone in the sun, acting as a beacon for others to come, to fall in love with her, then to own her.

So they did: the French, the Austrians, and finally, the Italians. These influences forever altered her culture, her language, and the minds of her people.

Today, the true heart of Venice remains in the diminishing population of "Those Who Remember." Those who still know their independence, still feel the power and importance of the mighty Republic, still taste her unique and delightful cuisine, and still fight to hold on to her native language.

Yes, Venice is today a part of Italy, but the last of her remaining Venetians want you to visit not thinking of her as Italy, but knowing of her...as Venice.

Patty Civalleri

TOUR YOUR OWN INTERESTS

PAGE NUMBERS

When you find yourself walking through the city, check the corresponding page to find interesting things as you stroll.

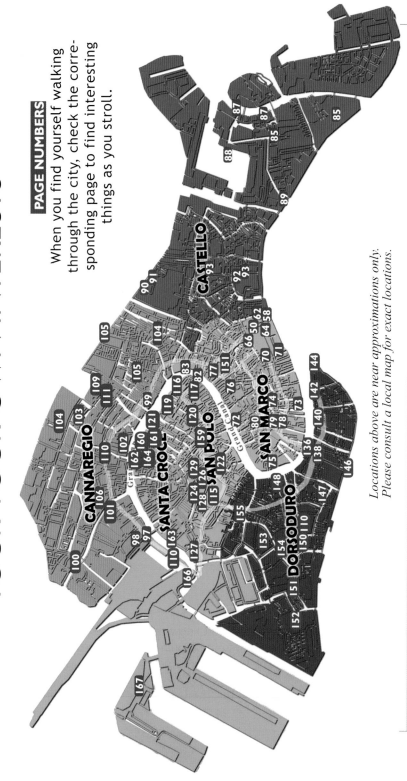

Locations above are near approximations only: Please consult a local map for exact locations.

Approximately 3 Miles

SEE IT YOUR WAY ~ FAQ'S

 If you are not sure where to start in Venice, here are Frequently Asked Questions to point you in directions that will help you to see more of what's fun for you - without wasting your short visit on the fluff that everyone thinks you SHOULD see.

Differences Between

A common misconception about Venice is that it is merely one more Italian city. But that just isn't so. Venice ruled for 1,000 years as an independent Republic, and became a part of Italy only 160 years ago. It still retains so many of its own traditions, food, even language from Austria.

Italy & Venice

Transportation

Cars, Trucks & Scooters
Much like the U.S., most cities in Italy run on engines and wheels.

Gondolas, Boats & Feet
Venice is the largest pedestrian (walking) city in the world. NO motorized vehicles, at all!

Food

Pizza & Pasta
Italy enjoys different specialties in each region. Pizza & Pasta are everywhere.

Seafood, Veggies
Venice is an island, so seafood is primary. And of course, Pizza & Pasta are also served for tourists.

Language

Cucchiaio = Spoon
Forchetta = Fork
Coltello = Knife

Vulgar Italian
Dante, the Father of Italian, wrote in the 'Vulgar' language of the people. This began the Italian language we know today.

More Latin-based
Venice had many outside influences. The Venetian language is more Latin-based, with some French, German and even Arabic thrown in.

Spoon = Scuger
Fork = Piron
Knife = Corteo

Public Transportation

Bus & Cab
Most cities in Italy rely heavily on buses, taxis and trains to move people throughout.

Vaporetto & Water Taxi
The Vaporetto "Water Bus" is the main form of public transport. The traghetto is a gondola that will take you directly across the Grand Canal.

Passageways

Streets & Freeways
Streets, roads, boulevards, and alleyways; paved with cobblestones, concrete and tar.

Canals & Bridges
Venice has over 400 foot bridges, one seemingly every block. These prevent wheeled vehicles from going anywhere at all.

VENICE IS SO PEDESTRIAN!

Even if you have been to Venice before, you may not have caught this extremely important point: **There are no cars. There are no scooters.** *(How completely un-Italian!)* **There are no bicycles. There are no roller skates.**

Besides wheeled package-delivery push-dollies, the only wheels you will see in Venice will be the ones you hear clacking down the cobblestone streets attached to the bottoms of tourists' suitcases.

Which brings up a good point: Don't pack heavy suitcases. Because not only will the cobblestones quickly shatter your wheels into a zillion splinters, you will most likely have to drag them up many foot-bridges - with steps up one side and down the other - before you reach your destination.

So it'll play out like this:

You'll arrive in Venice via plane, train, or bus. *(Cruise ship passengers, you won't need to read this part because your luggage will likely stay aboard the ship.)* **You** will drag your luggage to the Vaporetto station, then aboard a likely crowded Vaporetto *(water bus).* Then you'll drag your bags off the boat and onto the docks, then proceed through the cobblestone streets. The heavier your bags, the faster the wheels will break down. You'll drag them up one side of a bridge, then down the other. Fifty feet later, you'll do it again, and again. You'll probably get lost once or twice on the way, so more bridges.

By now, you'll be impatient, exhausted and probably angry at this ridiculous city. Eventually you will find your hotel or apartment, check in, and flop down, all the while wondering why so many people actually enjoy this crazy place!

Did You Know...

There are 118 islands in the city of Venice, with 403 bridges to connect the 177 waterways. The Grand Canal is the largest of these waterways.

Fear not. Go out and find a local bar. This will be easy, as there are usually several on each tiny block. Order a 'Spritz' *(it's a local hot-weather drink)* and relax, because you made it, you are now in Venice, the most incredible trip to the medieval times in today's world. A gelato will work wonders for the kids too!

STREETS & · · · · · · · · · · · ▶

CALLE = old Narrow Street

CAMPO = the open square in front of a Church; Italy calls them Piazzas

CAMPIELLO = a small Campo

CANAL = there are only 4 Canals in Venice: Grand Canal, Giudecca Canal, Cannaregio Canal, and San Piero Canal. All of the rest of the waterways are called a Rio or Riello.

CORTE = Leads to a Cul-de-Sac or dead end

FONDAMENTA = A street that runs along a Canal

PIAZZA = There is only one in Venice: Piazza San Marco. All others are called Campos or Campiellos.

PISCINA = Used to be a Pond, now paved

RAMO = Branches off of an important street

RIO TERRÀ = Used to be a Canal, but is now paved

RUGA = the Oldest Streets in Venice

SALIZADA = It was paved before all the other streets.

SOTOPORTEGO = a street that tunnels through a building

STRADA, VIA, and VIALE = Streets created during Austrian rule; wider than a Calle

20

• • • • • • • • • • • ▶ ADDRESSES

If you want to find a place based on its address, don't bother. The address numbering system in Venice has been done and re-done several times over, and you will lose hair trying to find your way by numbers.

Venice is divided into six Sestieri (or neighborhoods): San Marco, San Polo, Castello, Cannaregio, Dorsoduro, and Santa Croce. In the late 20th century, the numbering system was changed so that each Sestiere started with the number 1, and the numbers continued within that Sestiere until they ran out of buildings. So 215 San Polo is not a street address, but a building number within the Sestiere of San Polo. Cannaregio also has a 215, and Dorsoduro has a 215, etc.

Unfortunately, sometimes the numbers will wrap around corners, or at times the numbers may hop across a street before continuing. (Strange, I know.) Or if a Sestiere ends at 2559, and a new building gets built in the middle of the neighborhood, its number would be 2560, but it might be in between buildings 1202 and 1203. Good luck with this!

If you want to plan to meet someone, I would suggest that you say something like this: "Meet me in the Pizza Ristorante, Campo Saint Aponal, San Polo." Read it backwards like this: go to the San Polo Sestiere, find the Church of Saint Aponal, and go to the Pizza Restaurant in the Church's Campo. And I hope you don't go hungry while you wait.

BACKGROUND

ISLANDS IN THE LAGOON

COMUNE DI VENEZIA
1. Venice | Murano | Burano
2. Lido | Pellestrina
3. Favaro Veneto
4. Mestre | Carpenedo
5. Chirignago| Zelarino
6. Marghera

The city of Vennezia is made up of six communals (districts), each electing their own Mayor. The historic district where most tourists visit is the orange area (#1) above, and includes the islands of Venice, Murano, and Burano. The rest of the city proper is attached to the mainland and modern in their appearance. It is only the orange area where the buildings have been kept as close to its historical origin as possible, and as such, they attract tourists by the shipload.

Area #1 - the islands of Venice, Murano and Burano, are entirely pedestrian with no cars, buses, nor even scooters. The architecture of their buildings and homes cover the gamut from Byzantine to Venetian Gothic to Renaissance to Baroque. These 3 islands define the Historic District of Venice. As opposed to Lido Island (#2) and all of the others, which have modern buildings, street lights, vehicle traffic, and all the trappings of modern living.

Want a chain department store? Visit areas 2-6. Want a gondola ride? Visit area 1, and enjoy!

VENETIAN ISLANDS

There are many islands that dot the Venetian Lagoon. Most are non-accessible to visitors, as they may be privately owned or government owned for special uses. Over the past one-and-a-half millennia, however, they have been used as hide-outs, munitions storage, hospitals, and housing of quarantined individuals during the times of the plague. Today, the islands are used mainly for farming, fishing, monasteries, and general storage. This leaves but a few islands that are ***available for you to openly visit today.**

NORTHERN	CENTRAL	SOUTHERN
Buel del Lovo	Giudecca *	Lazzaretto Vecchio
Burano *	Sacca Fisola	Lido di Venezia *
Crevan	San Giorgio Maggiore *	Pellestrina
Cason	San Pietro di Castello	Poveglia
Montiron	San Secondo	Sacca Sessola
Isola dei Laghi	Sant'Elena	San Clemente
La Certosa	Tronchetto *	San Giorgio in Alga
La Cura Madonna del	Venice *	San Lazzaro degli Armeni
Lazaretto Nuovo *		San Marco in Boccalama
Mazzorbo *		San Servolo
Mazzorbetto		Sant'Angelo della Polvere
Monte dell'Oro		Santa Maria della Grazia
Motta dei Cunicci		Sottomarina
Motta di San Lorenzo		
Murano *		
Salina		
San Francesco del Deserto *		
San Giàcomo in Paludo		
San Michele Lazzaretto *		
Nuovo Santa Cristina		
Sant'Andrea		
Sant'Ariano		
Sant'Erasmo *		
Torcello *		
Vignoleoup		

THE VENICE LAGOON

MARCO POLO
INTERNATIONAL
AIRPORT

MURANO

CIMITERO DI SAN MICHELE
(ST. MICHAEL'S CEMETERY)

VENICE

GIUDECCA

TORCELLO

BURANO

MAZZORBO

SAN FRANCESCO

ST. ERASMO

LIDO INLET

LIDO

ADRIATIC SEA

BACKGROUND

KEY TO GETTING AROUND

5 KEY POINTS around the City:

48 San Marco *(St. Mark's Square)*
82 Ponte di Rialto *(Rialto Bridge)*
98 Ferrovia
138 Accademia
166 Piazzale Roma

These 5 KEY POINTS appear on the yellow signs *(opposite page)* that are posted all around the city. Having an idea of where these KEY POINTS are located will simplify your navigation through Venice.

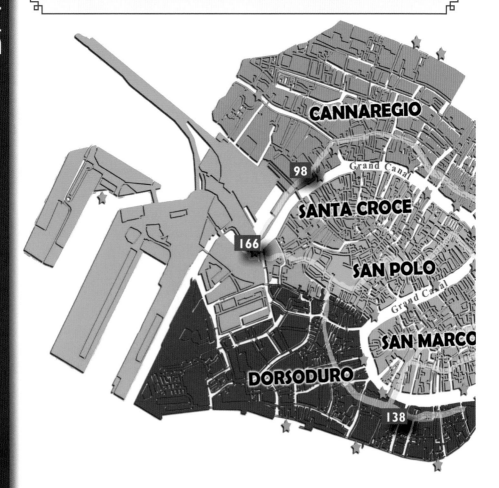

BACKGROUND

CANNAREGIO

Grand Canal

98

SANTA CROCE

166

SAN POLO

Grand Canal

SAN MARCO

DORSODURO

138

 =Vaporetto Stops

Approximately

Shaped like a Fish

The fish-shaped islands of Venice is divided into six districts, which they call "Sestieri." Each Sestiere has its own distinctive feeling, or 'personality.' It is not difficult to walk from one end of the city to the other and back. However, if you get weary towards the end of the day, simply jump aboard the Water Bus they call the "Vaporetto."

HINT: Yellow Lines & Yellow Signs

Notice the YELLOW LINE on the map below. This route can take you through many important areas of the city without getting lost.

[NOTE: There is no physical 'yellow line' actually painted on the street.]

You'll know you're on the right path when:

- You look up and see yellow signs on the walls pointing you to the KEY POINTS

- You will be in a strong flow of foot traffic.

- You will most likely be amidst lots of shops and restaurants.

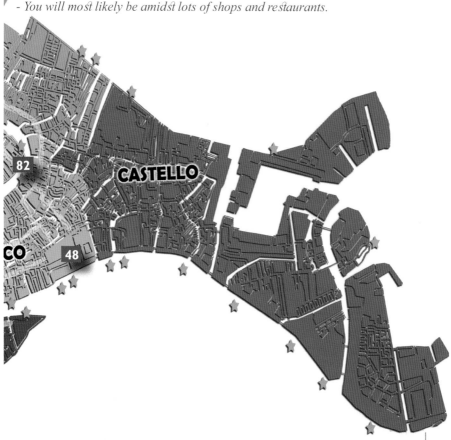

3 Miles

TOURISTS BEWARE!

BACKGROUND

If you eat, drink, or shop near Saint Mark's Square, you will probably over-pay, severely. A simple breakfast for 4 with coffee, juice, and a sweet roll could cost upwards of $100usd. Some places along the Grand Canal charge a $6 - $10 'table fee.' They may have a great view of the Square or the Grand Canal. Move on if you aren't ready to pay $100-$200pp for dinner. Many little hidden fees will quickly add up.

Do not eat or drink at the places that have a lot of glass in the front, perhaps a large door opening, and maybe even a person standing out-side trying to pull you in.

Look for restaurants that seem a bit dark. Maybe they won't even have windows that face the street. Their door will be small, unobtrusive. There will never be a person trying to pull you in. These little places are likely owned by a local resident. These places are quaint, and 'normal,' neither overly lit nor loud. They may serve items on the menu that you might not be familiar with. Try them anyway. After all, you are here to visit the real Venice, right?

Your Rewards:

Great food. In ALL cases. Quiet, quaint, Venetian. Sure most of them will in-clude pizza and pasta on their menu. But those are Italian-based tourist dish-es. As I write this, I am assuming that you are here to experience Venice - not America. I promise the seafood is exquisite. After all, you are on an island. The wines are fantastic! Start with baccalà as an appetizer *(cicchetti)* with an Aperol (sweet) or Compari (bitter) Spritz to wash it down and cool you off.

Bars: There are bars on virtually every block in Venice. Again, find the small, dark bars. They will all have a variety of appetizers on display. These are called cicchetti, *(pronounced chee-KEH-tee - it almost rhymes with spaghetti)*. If you don't know what to order, ask for baccalà, a cicchetti made from cod (taste's like a typical non-fishy white fish, like halibut), and served on bread. This paired with a Spritz, Prosecco, or Bellini, will truly make your day. Once you pay, take your drink and your cicchetti outside and find a place to stand. This is a normal Venetian social thing to do. Stand outside and talk to people while enjoying your drink.

Shopping: Wander away from San Marco, toward the Arsinale. Or cross the Rialto Bridge, and go deep into San Polo. Or cross the Accademia Bridge and walk the canals of Dor-soduro. Or pass the Rialto Bridge and walk down the wide Strada Nuova. These are places where you will find plenty of shopping, and WAY BETTER PRICES than anywhere near Saint Marks Square. To guarantee that you are purchasing authentic Venetian goods (not knock-offs), look for this Venezia Autentica sticker on the window of the shops. `282`

WHAT IS A SCUOLA GRANDE?

A Scuola Grande (Great School) was a neighborhood confraternity of non-noble citizens (men) in Venice, where their members could worship their patron saint. Instrumental in the teaching of music, a Scuola Grande also served many other purposes in the community. These included the distribution of food and clothing to the poor, the administration of the passing of dowries to daughters, the hosting of celebrations and festivals, and the burial of the homeless. Nobles were not allowed membership in a Scuola Grande, ergo membership for the citizens provided a forum for the locals to participate in the working affairs of the city. All Scuola Grande were closed down due to a Napoleonic decree, but re-opened later by the Austrians.

Today they serve different functions, as museums, sporting arenas, and even a performing arts theater. As you walk through the city, feel free to enter a Scuola Grande. You will immediately be impressed with the lavishly grand architecture and art within each.

Misericordia, now a museum

dei Carmini

San Rocco

San Marco, now a hospital

San Teodoro, now a theatre

Carità, now the Gallerie dell'Accademia

San Giovanni Evangelista

BACKGROUND

HISTORY

THE POWER OF THE VENICE REPUBLIC LASTED OVER 1,000 YEARS! BUT HOW?

This could only happen within a fairly closed, stable environment,
but why was Venice so stable? So peaceful? So Serene?
How/why did it evolve differently than the rest of Italy? Western Europe?

The falling Roman Empire was a primary trigger of Venice's birth. During the 400s Rome's failing budget and weakened power required that they remove military security and other assets from the northern areas of Italy. This act left hundreds of cities, towns, and settlements exposed and defenseless.

Thugs, thieves, and the destitute took this excuse to pillage the helpless towns and villages. Attila the Hun saw this as a convenient opportunity to conquer new territories. So he and his armies thundered through Northern Italy ransacking, burning and murdering as they went.

Locals from the city of **Altino** took their families and fled to the swampy, marshy islands in the lagoon. But first, they had to make the swamps habitable. So they built solid, stable islands on top of the marshland **35**.

While there, they mined and packaged the natural and abundant salt that existed in the islands. The trading of salt became a major source of revenue for them as they their homes emerged from the marshes.

The complex feat of building islands and mining salt required a strong sense of community and a powerful system of cooperation, not to mention strong back. Everyone had to contribute to the work, as slacking was not tolerated.

As their isolated island proved safe, more people wanted to live there. Everyone was required to contribute to the massive effort it took to create a city in the middle of the water.

Not only was a strong foundation built under the islands, but the strong - and remote - Venetian "stock" created a solid foundation for their upcoming Venice Republic.

Safety and remoteness was an attraction to many outsiders that had enough money to buy their way in. Another main source of funds came from mining abundant naturally available salt, and selling it to the outside world. This attracted more wealth and strong backs, which built more churches, created more islands, and so on.

On-going construction projects continually kept the Islanders employed. This process continued to spread money throughout the growing population, creating a self-perpetuating, stable, and independent economic system.

The new population created a decentralized system of governing by electing a "Doge" (similar to a Duke). A Doge held a lifetime term. With the help of a few layers of local decision-making committees, this Doge carried the power of the city. This was not a blood-driven aristocracy nor a monarchy. The population elected the Doges from among their own. A new Republic was born.

Life on the water meant that you became good at boat building. It was a driving force for life on islands. The Venetians became so good at building boats that they used these strong vessels to travel down the Adriatic Sea to visit places we know as Turkey, Croatia, Egypt, Africa, India, and China. This created a powerful trading economy. A large number of trading ships needed a strong system of security at sea, and so they created a visible profile of warships to protect the merchandise during transport.

Soon enough, they became the most proficient traders among foreign lands. They forged new trading paths far into the continents and also created new laws governing those paths. For example, all goods coming into and out of these new lands had to go through Venice. This amount of taxation gave Venice supreme power in all the port cities. All of this brought an unheard-of wealth and power to the city of Venice herself.

The year is now 1200ce. Venice is at an all-time high. The entire Western world was at its beck and call if they wanted to trade in the wealth of goods being brought from the other lands.

Venice had it all: a wealthy and stable economic system, the most influential trading system in the world, and the strongest maritime war fleet in existence at that time. They had it all.

BACKGROUND

SO WHAT HAPPENED TO IT?

The Venice Republic became known as "La Serenissima," or "The Most Serene Republic of Venice." These were not just words, but a "Brand" that captured the fact that Venice was not just a power to respect, but also that she had a mighty foundation of stability and peace. Everyone knew her as "La Serenissima."

In 1297, Venice made changes to their constitution, one that enabled citizens to define a Venetian aristocracy as those that could trace their heritage to a time before 1297. Once an aristocratic structure was defined, a caste system could be set into place. (Big mistake!)

An aristocratically-run lifestyle is expensive to support. As the once-wealthy city coffers emptied, they had to cut back. Their mindset had been transformed into one of peace, not war. War was for everyone else, not for the peace-loving Venice. So they cut back on shipbuilding, military crews, and overall defenses. By the late 1700s, the mighty fleet of 335+ ships and crew had been shrunken to 13 ill-maintained boats with a tiny crew of Croatian mercenaries.

What Venice forgot was that even though you don't plan to go to war; security and defense are still hugely necessary - if you have a lot to lose, as indeed Venice did.

In the 1790s, France viewed Venice as a sparkling gem to own. Napoleon saw the gap in Venetian security as an invitation for an easy takeover. And this he did. Running on a simple two-pronged plan, he effortlessly overtook the nearly non-existent Venetian military, and he convinced the local population to revolt against their ruling elite.

Venice fell like a Palazzo of cards.

The Napoleonic takeover in 1797 marked the end of a 1,000-year powerful and independent Republic. Venice managed to do something that no other country was able to do, and that was to maintain a position of stability for her own citizens for a hefty 1,000 years! For this, we should pay homage.

The Ping-Pong Ball of the Adriatic

Napoleon gave Venice to Austria as a gift of peace 235. But a few short years later France took Venice back from Austria during its own *(unsuccessful)* efforts to form the Napoleonic Kingdom of Italy. But when Napoleon was defeated in 1815, Austria took it back again.

For the next fifty years, Austria ruled Venice, then lost it one more time to France.

In the 1860s, Italy was pulling together all of the straggling city-states into a United Italy, and to show their support, France gave Venice to Italy to be included in this unification plan. The Venetians were resistant because they continued to see themselves as the proud **"La Serenissima,"** not merely as one more Italian city.

Epilog

Although Venice has since been transforming into a medieval tourist machine, the diminishing Venetian population still sees themselves as the mighty Venetian Republic, the Power of the Sea, La Serenissima.

Their Venetian language is now peppered with bits of the Austrian and French languages (and has since been virtually replaced by the Italian language), and their sea-based food has strong influences from France, Austria, and of course, Italy.

As you are eating and drinking your way through Venice, don't be too hasty to aid in this transformation. Be grateful that Venice was not lost in a city-damaging war, but has kept her sublime art, architecture, and culture for you to enjoy. Indulge in the remaining ancient wonders that are still the Great Venice: the funny street names, the great food, and the many kind smiles from the local Venetians who still deeply want to be remembered as **"The Most Serene Republic of Venice."**

BACKGROUND

How were the islands built?

During the 400s in the area that we know today as Northern Italy, the people were experiencing many changes causing an already faltering Roman Empire to accelerate its slow motion journey toward collapse. Many of the towns and villages in this northern region feared for their future as they watched the weakening of their once mighty Roman security blanket. This growing lack of security left them exposed to tormentors from the outside.

And predictably, they came. The Huns, Attila's formidable army, passed through and ransacked many of the townships and left a path of frightened townspeople scattered throughout the country-side.

Questioning their fate, many folks decided to move to the islands to escape the onslaught. This was a difficult decision because the hundreds of little islands in the Venetian lagoon were not much more than swampy, muddy, mushy, marshland. But flee they did, to the island of Torcello *(pronounced tor-CHEH-lo)*.

Did Attila the Hun Die 3 Times?

There are several 'official' accounts of Attila's death:

1. He got drunk and ate too much, while partying with his new wife Ildikó, and died in the night of epistaxis, a nosebleed.
2. His former wife Gudrun stabbed him to death.
3. He died after heavy drinking from esophageal varices which cause internal bleeding in the lower esophagus causing hemmoraging.

Current scholars seem to prefer the third account.

With limited materials, they created temporary shelters in which to live until they knew it was safe to return their families back to their original homes on the mainland. Most did return, but some enjoyed the marshy life on the island of Torcello and began to build.

This kind of swampy land is all that the early Venetians had to work with.

The marshy land was not easy to dominate. They had to find a way to not only strengthen the soft land, but also to claim more land from the surrounding waters. They built a wall of pilings to widely surround the swampy land that stuck up above the water, pounding them deep into the natural clay foundation. They filled this newly-created basin-like area with rocks, shells, and any other hard materials that could easily be acquired and transported. They covered this layer with another thick layer of dirt which they pounded to make it hard and flat.

What do Huns and Cats have in common?

Legend has it that the mainlanders moved to the islands because they heard that Attila the Hun's men were great soldiers on land, but like cats, they were afraid of the water. So fleeing to the islands seemed a pretty safe bet.

Meanwhile, back on the mainland, the rampaging army of Attila the Hun swept through creating the need for more mainland citizens to flee to the islands.

The population of the small island of Torcello grew quickly. They repeated this process, adding more islands as needed. These efforts left them with many pieces of usable land. Small foot-bridges were then added so that they could easily walk from one island to the other.

Eventually they decided to build a Church. So on March 25 at noon, in the year 421ce, the little city planted the first stone to create the Church of San Giacomo di Rialto, thus officially founding the new city of Venice.

Sack of Constantinople

Venice's Role in the 4th Crusade *(in a nutshell)*

The year was 1199. The 4th Crusade began in France when a group of knights at a jousting match fell to their knees and wept for their Holy Land which had been lost to Saladin in a prior war, and in the unsuccessful 3rd Crusade of 1187, a failed attempt at its recapture.

Swearing a holy oath, their boss, Count Thibaut of Champagne, sent six knights down to Venice to strike a deal to gain the help of La Serenissima (Venice) to help with a new campaign (the 4th Crusade) to win back access to their Holy Land. Venice would be happy to go along with this as long as they could replace the ruler of Constantinople, thereby paving a new route to better trading negotiations in the future. (Venice already had a grudge against the current Byzantine ruler; he had previously imprisoned some Venetians that lived peacefully in Constantinople.)

The Setup

In Venice, Doge (Duke) Dandolo carved out a deal as follows for this new Crusade:
- France would provide 33,500 men and 4,500 horses.
- Venice would provide ships, full crews, and one year of provisions for the men and their horses.
- Venice would also provide 50 fully-crewed war galleys to add to the French-laden fleet.
- Additionally, Venice wanted 50% of the spoils (50-50 partnership in the whole deal), plus 84,000 silver marks to pay for their hefty investment in the ships

The plan was not a direct one: they would sail down to Egypt to strike at the heart of the Muslim power base, led by the strong ambitions of an 80-year-old Doge Dandolo.

It took over two years to pull it together, and by 1203, the French returned, ready to go with only 10,000 troops (instead of the promised 33,500). Venice was not happy with this turn of events, and so charged France a hefty sum to cover the costs of their prep-work for the original-sized army.

Knowing they couldn't pay the debt, the French set out with the Venetians anyway. The shrewd Dandolo got an idea and made an offer that the Crusaders couldn't refuse: if while on their way to down to Constantinople they would conquer the city of Zara, Venice would forgive their massive debt.

The town of Zara was a Christian town, and many of the Crusaders didn't want to do it. But the French leaders felt they had no choice - they had that huge debt - so they sacked the poor little town.

This so angered Pope Innocent III in Rome who stated "How dare those Crusaders kill our people, when they themselves are supposed to be fighting in

BACKGROUND

The four life-sized bronze horses that are displayed atop the balcony of Saint Mark's Basilica are beautiful copies of the originals. The original horses that were 'acquired' from Constantinople are displayed on the other side of the wall, protected from the weather. You can visit them as you approach the external balcony.

the name of Christianity. You are excommunicated, all of you!" Meanwhile, the sacking ensued in Constantinople, with the French taking the land-side of the city, and the Venetians attacking on the waterside. Soon enough, the Venetians had the water-side under control, and so moved to the land side to assist the French. It was a long and tormented series of battles, but Dandolo, the aged but still crafty Venetian Doge, managed to lead his teams to victory.

Plenty of documentation exists that tell of the stories of the helter-skelter ways the French went about claiming their spoils from the city. And that the Venetians retained their civility as they took orderly inventories and moved treasures to their ships for the return home.

The spoils of war: walk around the side of Saint Mark's Basilica to see a collection of treasures brought to Venice from the sack of Constantinople.

VENICE in the year 1500

The woodcut map below was created by Jacopo de Barbari in the year 1500. Incredibly large at 9' x 4.5' [132.7 × 277.5 cm], the artist created it from six wood blocks using six large sheets of paper. The sheets of paper used were considered to be the largest ever to be produced in Europe until that time. There are thirteen known copies today, three of which live in the United States. This copy was acquired by The John R. Van Derlip Fund in 2010.

When Barbari created this bird's eye view in 1500, the top of the Campanile in St. Mark's Square had a flat top, as it was under repair at that time. Its pointed crown was replaced later, in 1514. The rest of the Square looks remarkably similar to the way it looks today, less the Napoleon wing on the west side which wasn't built until the 1800s.

Partial image of a woodcut map of Venice created by Jacopo de Barbari, c1500.

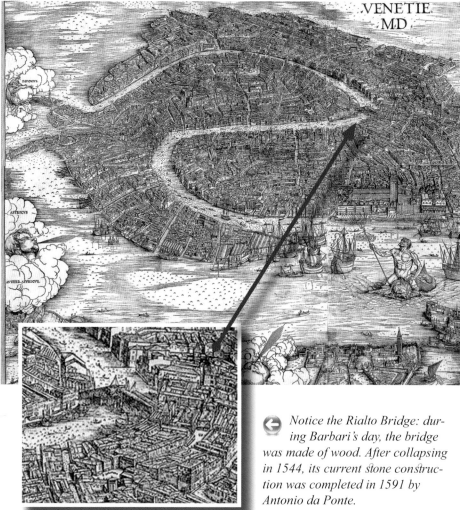

Notice the Rialto Bridge: during Barbari's day, the bridge was made of wood. After collapsing in 1544, its current stone construction was completed in 1591 by Antonio da Ponte.

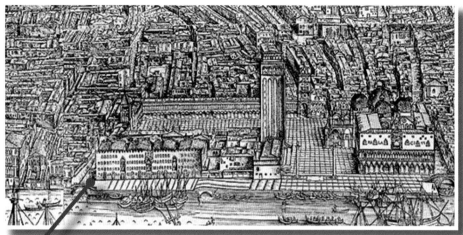

This image now lives in the Minneapolis Institute of Art in the United States.

Note the high wall around the Arsenale, and the overall wood construction of the facilities. The entire used to be heavily guarded to prevent spies, as the Arsenale produced the ships that were vital to the power that Venice held, both militarily and economically.

BACKGROUND

THE SESTIERE
6 DISTRICTS/NEIGHBORHOODS

SAN MARCO | CASTELLO | CANNAREGIO
SAN POLO | DORSODURO | SANTA CROCE

SAN MARCO SESTIERE

SAN MARCO

San Marco is the most common neighborhood (Sestiere) that visitors see in Venice because this is where St. Mark's Square is located. Because of this, it is also the most crowded of the Sestieri. But the rest of San Marco has plenty of other terrific sites to visit as well. Sure, it is the most crowded, but if shopping is what you are looking to do, then San Marco is the best Sestiere in Venice for you to be.

Saint Mark's Square contains many sites including the Basilica di San Marco, the Doge's Palace, the Bell Tower, the Clock Tower, Museo Correr, the National Museum of Archaeology, and the Marciana Library.

Sestiere

Basilica di San Marco **50**

The most luminescent church in the world, San Marco's Byzantine design combined with the endless mosaics will captivate you. The jewel-encrusted Pala d'Oro will mesmerise you. The story of stealing St. Mark's body from Egypt will amuse you, and the sheer size will amaze you.

Doge's Palace **58**

The Doge's Palace was the central seat of Venetian government. It contained the City Officials' offices as well as the Doge's apartment. It also housed a prison for 'soft' criminals. This grand hall, The Chamber of the Great Council, has been a place for formal meetings. The Torcher Chamber will send chills up your spine.

Bridge of Sighs **62**

The Bridge of Sighs (Ponte dei Sospiri) is a part of the Doge's Palace, and was designed in 1600 by Antonio Contino, the nephew of Antonio di Ponte, the man who designed the Rialto Bridge not ten years prior. This enclosed bridge was built to connect the prisoner interrogation rooms in the Doge's Palace to the New Prison 36 feet across the little Rio di Palazzo below. Location: attached to the east side of the Doge's Palace

Bell Tower (Campanile) **64**

The San Marco Bell Tower (the Campanile) began construction during the 1100's atop what was previously the site of a watchtower. All bell towers in the Veneto Lagoon area were modelled after this original tower. Standing 384 feet in height, the city has seen fit to include an elevator to whisk you to the top - no stairs to climb!

SAN MARCO

Sestiere

SAN MARCO

Sestiere

66 Clock Tower

The Clock Tower of San Marco (the Moors' Clock Tower) was commissioned by Agostino Barbarigo, the Venice Doge in 1493. The feeling among the Senate members at the time was that because Venice was considered to be the greatest Maritime Power in the Western World.

70 Museo Correr

The Museo Correr resides in the Napoleonic Wing of Saint Mark's Square, the wing directly across from the face of the Basilica. The building retains many of the hallmarks of the age of Bonaparte: the architecture, decoration, frescoes, and furnishings of neoclassical taste give an important testimony to the culture and languages of that era.

71 Museum of Archaeology

The Venice Archaeological Museum is legitimately defined as "the heir of the ancient Public Statuary of the Most Serene Republic of Venice." It is essentially a collection of ancient statuary from as far back as the first century. Included are items from ancient Rome and Greece, such as sculptures of marble and bronze.

72 Fortuny Palace

Once owned by the Pesaro family, this large Gothic palazzo was transformed by Mariano Fortuny into his own atelier of photography, stage-design, textile-design, and painting. The building retains the rooms and structures created by Fortuny, together with his personal tapestries and collections.

Musica aPalazzo 73 (Music in a Palace)

Overlooking the Grand Canal, Musica aPalazzo is a creative way to enjoy and share Chamber Opera, where each scene unfolds in a different room within the palace. This approach gives the audience a new way to experience the story. An excellent way to spend an evening in Venice.

La Scala del Bovolo 74

Formally known as Scala Contarini del Bovolo, this spiral tower sits humbly near Campo Manin in the San Marco Sestiere. Being one of the taller buildings in the neighborhood, it enjoys a splendid 360° panoramic view of glorious Venice from the top.

Palazzo Grassi 75

Along with the Punta della Dogana (on the Sestiere Dorsoduro), the Palazzo Grassi was inaugurated as a Contemporary Art Museum, certainly a major museum of Venice. The exhibits are changed periodically, so a new visit to this old building may be well worth your while.

Ponte dell'Accademia 136

From atop this bridge you will enjoy some of the best views of the Grand Canal in both directions. This wooden beauty will transport you from the bustling crowds of San Marco to the quieter, more locally enjoyable side of Dorsoduro.
NOTE: The details of the Accademia Bridge are in the Dorsoduro section of this book.

SAN MARCO

Sestiere

45

SAN MARCO

Sestiere

76 Teatro Goldoni

*Performed by Teatro Stabile del Vene-
to, are a selection of plays to amuse,
most of which were the antics of the
playwright Carlo Goldoni (1707-
1793).*

*Carlo Goldoni's theatrical humor was
loved by all, and warranted a statue in
his honor. You can view this sculptured
monument in the Campo S. Bortolomi,
near the Rialto Bridge.*

77 Scuola Grande Confraternita di S.Teodoro - I Musici Veneziani

*This building was converted into a
theatre of Musical Performances and
serves as a striking example of the
basilica architecture of old. Originally
built in 1258, it was dedicated to San
Teodoro, the Patron Saint of Venice
before the relics of Saint Mark were
stolen from Egypt and brought to
Venice.*

78 Teatro La Fenice

*This Theatre is one of the most famous
theatrical landmarks in all of Venice.
It has been home to some of the most
famous performers, including Verdi,
Stravinski, Rossini, Bellini, and Donizetti. Founded in 1792, La Fenice,
"the Phoenix," is the grandest of live
performance theatres in the city of
Venice. This sumptuous neo-classically
designed theatre seems to be in perfect
harmony with the orchestral gifts that
it produces.*

Museum of Music 79

A little-known gem in the San Marco Sestiere is the Museum of Music. It lives within the converted San Maurizio Church, and is an elegant surprise. An array of centuries-old stringed instruments are deliciously displayed throughout. Additionally, the museum offers an excellent variety of sheet music for purchase for both stringed classics as well as modern compositions.

Chiesa di Santo Stefano 80

One of the famous Leaning Towers of Venice, Santo Stefano was built in 1294, but had to be rebuilt several times over the centuries. Bull fights were held in antiquity in her Campo in front of the Church. She is but one of several leaning towers in Venice. Can you find them all?

The Rialto Bridge 82

(Ponte di Rialto)

This bridge is the most recognizable landmark in Venice. Laced with jewelry and high-end souvenir shops, it offers the most picturesque views of the Grand Canal. It was created to facilitate the movement of fresh foods from the Rialto Marketplace on one side of the bridge to the San Marco Sestiere on the other side.

Fondaco dei Tedeschi 83

The Shopping Mall with a gift on top: The finest in European big label designers all have shops here. An elegant ground-floor lounge will break up your shopping monotony. But don't stop there. Take the **RED escalator** *to the top and go outside to get the best view, from the Grand Canal to the Arsenale! Located next to the Rialto Bridge. This little secret is not widely known by tourists.*

ST. MARK'S SQUARE

Saint Mark's Square is the most visited spot in the entire city of Venice. There is so much to do and see here, that most tourists forget about the awe and mysteries that await throughout the rest of the city.

The splendid Church of San Marco is well worth a visit. A ride to the top of the Bell Tower (the Campanile) offers unprecedented views, while a lesser-known tour to the top of the Clock Tower affords a different perspective. The Correr museum and the National Museum of Archaeology will teach you about the history of the area. The luxurious Doge's Palace is the residence of

SAN MARCO

Sestiere

Bell Tower (Campanile)

Correr Museum

National Museum of Archaeology

VENICE

all of the past Doges (Dukes) of the city, and it holds the prison where Casanova was incarcerated **228**. The picturesque Bridge of Sighs is a historically-charged site. Spend a full day in this area, then move on to the rest of the city. If you have been here in the past, you'll find many ways to avoid the mobs to get to the more interesting sites all throughout Venice.

Sestiere San Marco

Clock Tower

St. Marks Basilica

Casanova's Prison Cell

Bridge of Sighs

Doge's Palace (Palazzo Ducale)

Ponte della Paglia

BASILICA di SAN MARCO

SAN MARCO

An evening in Saint Mark's Square will reward you with a nicely lit view of one of the most glorious Basilicas in the world.

Sestiere

The Basilica that you see here today is actually the third church to be built on this space. The first iteration was built in 828 when the relics of Saint Mark were brought to Venice from Egypt. Archaeological remains show that it had a much smaller footprint, but the exact dimensions are lost to time. Pieces of the existing ruins have become part of the crypt that is still in use today. The

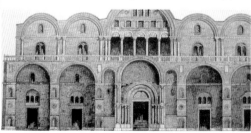

second iteration was built in 976 after the lynching of the Doge Pietro IV Candiano burned down both the Doge's Palace as well as the Church. The third and most recent iteration was created in 1063 on top of the prior foundation using some of the walls of the previous church in the same location. It was created with a strong Greek Byzantine architectural style. This church was conceived using the Basilica of the Twelve Apostles in Constantinople as the model. The church was consecrated in 1094.

The Story of Saint Mark

And so it began. Mark was one of Christ's 70 disciples, who during his travels once passed through the Veneto area. Later he went to Alexandria, in present-day Egypt, to continue his charitable works, including the founding of the Church of Alexandria. He died in Egypt around 68ce.

Fast-forward nearly eight centuries, to the year 828. Venice decided to send some merchants down to Egypt to find the relics of Saint Mark and bring them back to Venice. Once they found him, they put him in a cart covered with pork to keep the Muslims, who couldn't touch pork, from inspecting the contents of the cart. They successfully brought him back, and built a church in his honor, and have kept his relics here ever since.

As the legend continues, the ship carrying his relics was overtaken by a severe storm at sea. It is said that St. Mark appeared to the captain telling him to lower his sails. He complied, saving his ship, the crew, and the relics. This story is depicted in the mosaic above the left entrance door.

"Stealing Saint Mark's Body" Tintoretto, c. 1562-1566. Tintoretto created this painting as one of three that were to hang in the San Marco Scuola Grande in Venice. He painted it as if the merchants had found St. Mark's actual body, but the real story states that they went to fetch his relics. After all, he had been dead for nearly 800 years at that point. This painting can now be enjoyed in the Gallerie dell'Accademia in Venice.

SAN MARCO

Sestiere

Basilica di SAN MARCO

SAN MARCO

Acres of Gold Mosaics

There are so many spectacular things to see in the Basilica di San Marco. The single most spectacular thing - among many spectacular things - is the accumulation of mosaics throughout its interior space. Indeed there are over 86,000 square feet of mosaics covering the walls, floors, and ceilings - which is equal to two acres of coverage!

These mosaics have been created over the course of 800+ years. They tell biblical stories: old and new testaments, allegorical stories, and stories of Christ. Equally as interesting are the stories within the mosaics that beautifully document the history of Venice.

This is a tiny sampling of the mosaics you will see in the Basilica di San Marco.

Sestiere

SAN MARCO

Sestiere

The four life-sized **bronze horses** that are displayed outside atop the balcony of Saint Mark's Basilica, over-looking the square, are merely beautiful copies of the originals. The original horses that were 'acquired' from Constantinople **36** are displayed on the other side of the wall, protected from the weather. You can visit them as you approach the external balcony.

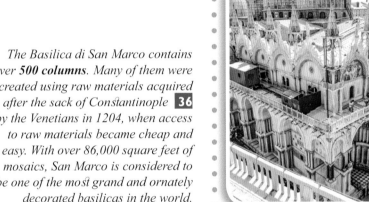

The Basilica di San Marco contains over **500 columns**. Many of them were created using raw materials acquired after the sack of Constantinople **36** by the Venetians in 1204, when access to raw materials became cheap and easy. With over 86,000 square feet of mosaics, San Marco is considered to be one of the most grand and ornately decorated basilicas in the world.

One of the mosaics, the **PALA D'ORO,** is considered to be the highest form of the expression of Byzantine genius reaching towards God. This "retable" sits in its original position behind the altar and contains the relics of Saint Mark. The gold sheet is encrusted with 1,927 pieces of precious stones and gems, and trimmed with 250 pieces of cloisonné enamel. Although it is too big to fit in our pages, the main center portion is depicted **on the next page.**

BASILICA DI SAN MARCO
The interior of the Basilica di San Marco is one of the most impressive Gothic Churches in the world. Gold tile mosaics cover the walls and ceiling and tell historical accounts of the city of Venice.

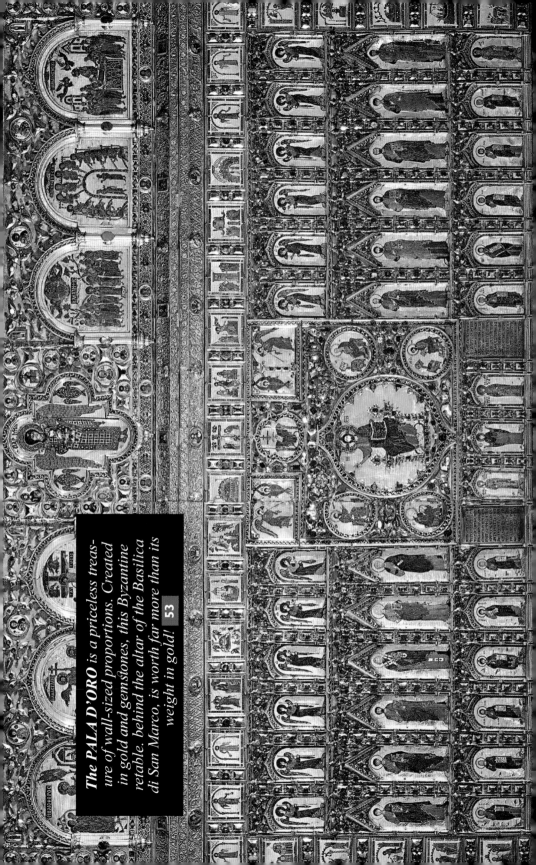

The PALA D'ORO is a priceless treasure of wall-sized proportions. Created in gold and gemstones, this Byzantine retable, behind the altar of the Basilica di San Marco, is worth far more than its weight in gold! 53

SAN MARCO

Sestiere

Doge's Palace

DOGE'S PALACE

SAN MARCO

The Doge's Palace lies along the Lagoon next to San Marco.

The Doge's Palace was the central seat of Venetian government. It contained the City Officials' offices as well as the Doges' apartment. It also housed a prison for 'soft' criminals. The Hall of the Maggior Consiglio now serves as a gathering place for important meetings.

Sestiere

What is a Doge?

Simply put, a Doge was a Duke, but not the same as an English Duke. This was not an inherited title, it was an elected position held for the remainder of his life. The Doge was the Chief Magistrate of the City. He was the leader of the Most Serene

How to Address a Doge

Every royal position has its traditions of title. To speak to a Doge, you would address him as:

"My Lord the Doge" or
"Most Serene Prince" or
"His Serenity"
  Mrs. Doge would be called a "Dogaressa"

Republic of Venice (La Serenissima). Since the forming of the Venetian Republic in 697ce, there have been 120 Doges, each of whom was elected to carry out their Ducal responsibilities for the remainder of their life - no matter how short that life was to become. A Doge's activities were limited to the confines of the Doge's Palace and to Saint Mark's Basilica for the remainder of his term/

A Gritty End

In 1534, the Doge of Venice was Andrea Gritti. His unglamorous death is the stuff of legends. It seems that during the Christmas Eve dinner in 1538, Gritti, then 83 years old, gorged himself on a tureen of bean soup and skewered eels. He died after a four-day torturous bout of indigestion.

life. There were, however, random ceremonial and diplomatic occasions when his presence was required outside of these two buildings. One ceremony that was most favored by the Doges was the Festa della Sensa 272, held annually on Ascension day. During this ceremony, the Doge would don his royal robes and board the Bucintoro 256 to enjoy the prestige of being rowed through the

Lagoon, from San Marco to Lido Isle. Surrounded by rowers in every kind of human-powered boat, the Doge would conduct the ceremony of the wedding of Venice to the Sea by tossing a ring into the waters of the lagoon. Pomp and music accompanied the entire trip. How nice it must have been to get out of the house for a day!

SAN MARCO

Doge's Palace

Within the walls of the Palace are prison cells where they kept criminals of 'soft' crimes. The famous lover Casanova escaped from one such as this.

The Torture Chamber, where they forcibly extracted knowledge from captives, sits next to the Magistrate's office where he could hear their screams of pain.

CIAO

The word "Ciao" *(pronounced 'chow')* comes from the word 'schiavo' *(pron 'skee-AH-vo" in Italian)*, or sciavo *(pron 'shee-AH-vo' in Venetian)*. Eventually the 'v' was dropped. Because schiavo means 'Slave,' it originally translated to "I am your slave," or "I am at your service." Today it is simply used as a casual and friendly 'hi' and 'bye.'

Samples of weaponry used over a millenia-and-a-half are kept in the Armory room within the Doge's Palace. Today, they are beautifully displayed for all to see. In addition, the attic exhibits a larger cache of weapons, full suits of armor, and a considerable variety of field weapons.

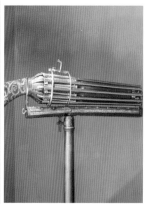

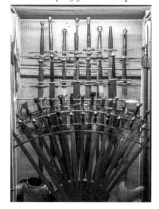

Sestiere

If you take the 'Secret Itineraries' tour, you may emerge from the wardrobe at the far corner of this room. This is one example of the many secret passages hidden throughout the palace.

The balcony is a great spot to enjoy the late afternoon sun over Piazza San Marco.

There is a labyrinth of rooms and chambers within the walls of the Palace. Among these are the Chamber of 40, the Guarientor, the Chambers of the Great Council, the Scrutino, the Criminal Court-room, the Magistrate's Chamber, the Scarlet Chamber, the Shield room, the Grimani room, the Erizzo, the Stuco room, the Vault room, the Philosopher's room, the Audience room, the Ante-Audience room, the Equerries room, the 4-Doors room, the Council Chamber, the Senate Chamber, the Chamber of the Council of 10, the Compass room, the Chamber of Censors, the Chamber of the State Advocacies, the Scrigno room, the Chamber of the Navy Captains, the Armoury, the Prisons, and yes, even a Chamber of Torment.

The Doge, even though confined to this building for the remainder of his life, rarely ran out of things to do in this many-chambered dungeon Palace.

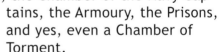

"The Giant's Staircase" can be found at the courtyard entrance. Atop the stairs are the two giant statues of Mars and Neptune, representing Venice's power over both the land and the sea. Statues by Jacopo Sansovino, 1554-67.

SAN MARCO

Sestiere

BRIDGE OF SIGHS
(part of the Doge's Palace)

The Bridge of Sighs *(Ponte dei Sospiri)* was designed in 1600 by Antonio Contino, the nephew of Antonio di Ponte who designed the Rialto Bridge not ten years prior. This enclosed bridge was built to connect the interrogation rooms in the Doge's Palace to the New Prison 36 feet across the little Rio di Palazzo below it.

This iconic Renaissance structure was created from white Istrian marble (metamorphosed limestone), with stone-latticed windows and lined with gargoyles to ward away evils. From the inside looking out through the latticed windows, the world looks positively unreachable.

In fact, there is more online prattle regarding its name, than there is about the magnificence of the bridge itself.

As is illustrated in novels, poetry, and the movies, the Bridge of Sighs is all about romance. The general belief is that if you cross under the bridge at sunset, your love will be eternal. This is great for the Gondoliers at the end of the day, as tourists line up to take the ride that will ensure their everlasting love.

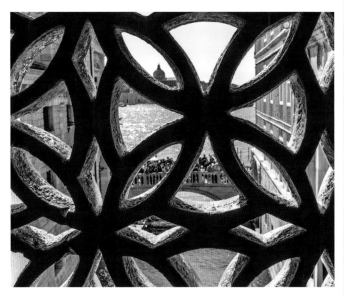

Some think the name comes from a poem written by Lord Byron, depicting the sighs of lovers as they pass beneath this romantic bridge. Some feel that the name came from the sighs of despair that came from prisoners when they took one last look out the latticed windows as they walked that last excruciatingly slow walk, while being escorted from the courtroom across the bridge to their prison cell.

But no matter how you look at it, the Bridge of Sighs is a glorious and unexpected sight, as you look down the waterway to see its intricate beauty dangling over the canal.

The outside of the bridge bears an uncharacteristically romantic image, as compared to its stark, bare interior.

Bridge of Faces

If you look closely at this exceptional example of Baroque architecture, you will see 20 faces spread around the outside of the Bridge of Sighs. Many Venetians have attached similar ugly or angry faces to the outside of their homes to ward off evil spirits. Holding with tradition, Contino placed these types of faces on the bridge to protect it as well.

SAN MARCO

BELL TOWER of SAN MARCO

The San Marco Bell Tower *(the Campanile)* began construction during the 1100s atop what was previously the site of a watchtower. All bell towers in the Veneto Lagoon area were modelled after this original tower.

Standing 384 feet in height, the city has seen fit to include an elevator to make it easy for you to get to the top.

The tower has felt the pain of many disasters, including repeatedly being struck by lightning, and eventually collapsing in 1902.

> ## Eye in the Sky
> In 1609, Galileo Galilei showed his new telescope to the Doge Antonio Priuli at the top of this Campanile.

- **1388** - Lighting Strike
- **1403** - Top part burned when a celebration got out of hand
- **1511** - Earthquake
- Lightning Strikes 7 more times over the next five centuries
- **1902** - The tower collapsed. **266** The sound of bricks hitting the bells warned bystanders to move clear.

Four of the five bells in the tower were destroyed during this collapse. Afterwards, the city officials met to decide whether or not to rebuild the tower.

It was unanimous that the tower should be rebuilt. But as is common with most political issues, the decision was split between those that wanted it to be a duplication of the original tower, and those who wished for a newer design. Due to the sentimentality held for the original design as well as the history it held, they decided to rebuild to the original design, but this time, it would be stronger, sturdier, and safer.

Sestiere

Language of the Bells

Bell towers were helpful in many ways, including a great means of security, as the views were wide ranging. Most of the bell towers in the city had their own tone, key, or chord to signify which church was ringing.

The bells themselves were a solid form of communication throughout the city. The five bells within the Bell Tower of San Marco had their own language, which was understood by everyone in the city.

- **The Marangona** bell would signal when the carpenters at the Arsesnale should begin and end work each day. It rang in the key of 'A'.
- **The Nona** rang the Noontime bell. It rang in the key of 'B'.
- **The Trottiera** bell would tell the Maggior Consiglio (Grand Council) of the city to set their horses to a trot, so they would not be late for a meeting at the Doge's Palace. It rang in the key of 'C'.
- **The Mezza Terza** bell would tell the Senate to get to their meeting, also that religious services were to begin. It rang in the key of 'D'.
- **The Renghiera** (or Maleficio) bell would tell the city that an execution was taking place. It rang in the key of 'E'.

On special occasions, they were rung in unison.

Of these five bells, the Marangona is the only original surviving bell. The other four bells were destroyed during previous disasters. Later, Pope Pius X had those four bells rebuilt and replaced after the tower collapsed in 1902.

> ### Video Games
> The San Marco Bell Tower can be found in the video game "Assassin's Creed." Set in the 1490s, characters scale the tower to get a birds-eye view of ancient Venice.

Left: The view from the top of the Bell Tower shows us the rooftop of the Doge's Palace and the curved expanse of the island. **Right:** *The San Marco Bell Tower photo was taken from a window inside the Museum Correr, across the square.* 70

SAN MARCO

Sestiere

CLOCK TOWER of SAN MARCO

SAN MARCO

Sestiere

History

The Torre dell'Orologio - Clock Tower of San Marco - *(the Moors' Clock Tower)*, was commissioned by Agostino Barbarigo, the Venice Doge in 1493. The feeling among the Senate members, at the time, was that because Venice was considered to be the greatest Maritime Power in the world, then she should at least have an accurate clock, visible to passing ships, that would suitably represent this position of honor.

The structure/housing was probably designed by Mauro Coducci, and the inner mechanisms were created by the father-and-son team of Giampaolo and Giancarlo Rainieri. The Clock Tower was finished in 1499, at which

Rumor Had It

For centuries, a popular rumor circulated, stating that after the clock was finished, the Senate members, who so completely admired this clock, blinded the clock makers to keep them from duplicating this treasure elsewhere. But we know now that this was untrue, because the clock makers' families lived within the clock tower and handled its maintenance on an ongoing basis. It would have been quite impractical to blind them before hiring them for this lifelong position.

point; the family Rainieri moved into the tower, taking the positions as guardians and maintenance managers of the Clock. This housing agreement was upheld for the maintenance personnel for the next 500 years.

Fixes and Upgrades

Over the centuries, the clock tower has suffered 'injuries' from mother nature and by time itself, requiring several updates along the way.

For the first ten years, the tower stood alone before they added two bays on each side for support. In the 1700s Giorgio Massari added eight columns across the bottom for added support and the rails across the top of the side bays. In the 1800s the old wooden stairs were replaced with an iron staircase that spirals its way to the top of the tower.

Because of its nearly perfect accuracy, the city of Venice decided to name this clock, as the Official Time Keeper of the city, and it is by this clock that all clocks in the city are set.

SAN MARCO

Sestiere

Clock Tower of San Marco

The view of Saint Mark's from the top of the Clock Tower.

The two bronze bell-ringers were originally called 'Giants.' But as the bronze eventually turned black, people began calling them Moors; hence the clock's nickname is now the Moors' Clock Tower.

Looking down upon the alley behind the tower, from a beautiful rose port hole 3/4 up the clock tower.

With Roman numerals representing each hour, and Western Arabic numerals representing each five minute interval, these giant wheels turn to display the time to the onlookers in St. Mark's Square below..

View from an upper port hole.

Upon reaching the top of the tower, you will emerge from this odd portal onto the rooftop.

The city's symbol of the Winged Lion keeps watch over the people of Venice.

The Virgin Mary sits with the baby Jesus on her lap. Occasionally this statue will come forward, rotate, then return to its original position.

During Ascension week the 3 Magi will come out from a hidden door, circle around Mary, then return through another hidden door.

The outer ring shows 24 hours in Roman numerals, with a 'sun' hand pointer. The middle ring shows the current sign of the Zodiac. The inner circle depicts the phases of the moon.

A peek through one of the lower port holes.

The metal staircase replaced the original wooden stairs in the 1800s. This is where you will start the tour up the clock tower.

MUSEO CORRER

The Museo Correr resides in the Napoleonic Wing of Saint Mark's Square, the wing directly across from the face of the Basilica. The building retains many of the hallmarks of the age of Bonaparte: the architecture, decoration, frescoes, and furnishings of neoclassical taste give an important testimony of the culture and languages of that era.

The Correr Museum takes its name from Teodoro Correr (1750-1830), a nobleman of an ancient Venetian family, an attentive and passionate collector. At his death in 1830, he donated his art collection to the city,

Teodoro was a diligent collector of Venetian memorabilia of his age. As it turns out, this was a critical time in Venetian history: Napoleon ended the 1,000-year-long Venetian Republic **234**, and the Austrians came in to run the city based on Napoleonic decree.

This changed everything in Venice: from the tastes in art and architecture, to fashion and food. Correr was instrumental in gathering items that were both demonstrative and explanatory references to this catastrophic jolt away from the traditions of the Venetian Republic, and into a new age of Austrian rule.

The museum contains a small cafe where snacks and wine can be enjoyed, while savoring a spectacular secret view over-looking the entire Saint Mark's Square.

ARCHAEOLOGICAL MUSEUM

The Venice Archaeological Museum is legitimately defined as "the heir of the ancient Public Statuary of the Most Serene Republic of Venice."

It is essentially a collection of ancient statuary from as far back as the 1st century.

Included are items from ancient Rome and Greece such as statuary of important members of the Roman military, vases, coins of the age, tapestries, and portraits.

The collection was started with donations by Cardinal Domenico Grimani in 1523, and lives in the wing adjacent to Saint Mark's Basilica.

Domitian, c. 84-96 AD, 16th century bust

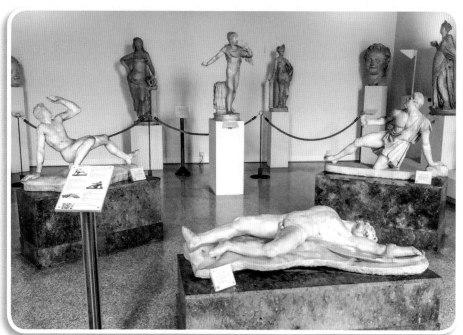

A room displaying classical sculptures in the Venice National Archaeological Museum,

SAN MARCO

FORTUNY PALACE

Once owned by the Pesaro family, this large Gothic palazzo in
Campo San Beneto was transformed by Mariano Fortuny into
his own atelier of photography,
stage-design, textile-design, and
painting. The building retains
the rooms and structures created by Fortuny, together with
his personal tapestries and his
own collections. The working
environment of Mariano Fortuny
is represented through precious
wall-hangings, paintings, and
the famous lamps – all objects
that testify to the artist's inspiration, and still give count of his
eclectic work and of his presence
on the intellectual and artistic
scene, at the turn of the 19th
century.

The Fortuny Museum was donated to the city in 1956 by
Henriette, Mariano's wid-
ow. The collections within
the museum comprise an
extensive number of piec-
es and materials, which
reflect the various fields
investigated in the artist's
work. These are organized
under certain specific
headings: painting, light,
photography, textiles, and
grand garments.

Sestiere

MUSICA aPALAZZO

Musica aPalazzo is a 'traveling' opera. This means that each scene is carried out in a different suite, within the splendid Venetian Palazzo Barbarigo Minotto.

After each scene, the audience gets up and moves to another room in the Palace to see the next scene. This goes on during the length of the show.

Having a palace for a venue lends itself to this unique approach for live theater. It gives the audience more of a sense of involvement, rather than sitting in a single spot for the evening.

The performers skillfully utilize the Baroque decor set in each room, using the spaces in clever and interactive ways.

SAN MARCO

LA SCALA del BOVOLO

Sestiere

Formally known as La Scala Contarini del Bovolo *(snail)*, this spiral tower sits humbly near Campo Manin in the San Marco Sestiere. Being one of the taller buildings in the neighborhood, it boasts a splendid 360° panoramic view of glorious Venice.

Commissioned by the Contarini family in the late 1400s to adorn their adjacent Palazzo, its name was derived from its shape of a snail's shell; Bovolo is the Venetian word for 'snail.'

La Scala del Bovolo is a bit difficult to find as it is buried within the labyrinthian alleyways so famous to Venice.

But don't give up, as the 80-step climb to the tower's top will reward you with a divine scene of the entire city.

In 1979, American Actor Roger Moore was chased up this tower in Eon Production's "Moon Raker," part of the 007 James Bond series of books by Ian Fleming.

"The iconic spiral staircase most impressive and valuable in Venice is a perfect synthesis of different styles: Renaissance (for the use of some elements such as the capitals), Gothic (for the construction technique), and Venetian-Byzantine (for the form)" ~ Palazzo Contarini del Bovolo

PALAZZO GRASSI

SAN MARCO

> "My sincere wish is that the contemporary art center, consisting of Palazzo Grassi and Punta della Dogana, shall remain truly contemporary. This impetus is a matter of great importance for me, but also for Venice, a city, which has always inspired the best of creativity."
>
> ~*François Pinault*

Palazzo Grassi and her sister museum, Punta della Dogana **144**, across the Grand Canal are the showplaces for the finest in contemporary art. Beginning with the Pinault collection, the organization prides itself on its relationships with the artists themselves. Several exhibits were designed specifically for the spaces within, giving them a unique life that can not be found elsewhere. Included in the space is a 250-chair auditorium used for performances, concerts, and screenings. Palazzo Grassi is also a showcase for Biennale art.

Sestiere

The inside of Palazzo Grassi will be a wonderful surprise, as artists find ways to set their exhibits among the already highly decorous interior spaces.

GOLDONI THEATRE

SAN MARCO

Owned by the Vendramins, a noble Venetian family in the 1700s, this building has presented beautiful operatic performances for three centuries.

In a time when the rest of Europe was into plays and playwrights, Venice pumped up the volume on operatic performances. The nobles of the city became quite competitive in the lavish construction and interior decorations of their theaters, and soon the rest of Europe became envious.

Once again, Venice found another arena in which to reign: operatic theater. And at that she clearly ruled.

Sestiere

SAN TEODORO
Scuola Grande

The Scuola Grande di San Teodoro is today a theatre of performing arts.

Originally built in 1258. it was dedicated to San Teodoro, who was the Patron Saint of Venice before the relics of Saint Mark **50** were stolen from Egypt and brought to Venice. The rooftop features San Teodoro flanked by four angels, sculpted by Bernardo Falcon in the late 1600s.

The Confraternity carried out their charitable works until 1807 when the Napoleonic Decree suppressed the business of the Confraternities.

In 1960, it was once again transformed with a perpetual-use license and today hosts regular performances of light opera, Baroque and Classical music.

SAN MARCO

Sestiere

77

TEATRO LA FENICE

Founded in 1792, La Fenice, "The Phoenix," is the grandest of live performance theatres in the city of Venice.

The sumptuous neoclassical theatre is in perfect harmony with the orchestral gifts that it produces. In the original version of the building, the box seats that cover the walls were somewhat similar to what you see today. The red seats in the center of the room were missing; the entire floor was open where lower-cost ticket holders could stand during performances.

From operas to Baroque to Classical music, the acoustics within La Fenice are pitch perfect.

Sublime performances of the greatest composers in the world have graced this stage. These have included Rossini, Donizetti, and the vivacious Verdi, among many others.

The 1,000-seat theatre can accommodate a 98-member orchestra and a 66-member opera chorus. It boasts approximately 100 performances each year, and an extravagant list of world-renowned composers, performers, and conductors.

The reference to the Phoenix rising from the ashes comes from the destruction of the theatre due to three fires. The first occurred in 1774, then in 1836, and finally the horrific arson fire of 1996.

The reopening of the theatre in 2004 after the latest fire, featured lavish productions of Wagner, Beethoven, and Igor Stravinski.

MUSEUM OF MUSIC

If stringed instruments are your thing, this gem of a museum will be a place for you to spend some of your treasured Venetian time.

Tucked shyly behind the leaning tower of Santo Stefano, the Museum of Music is a rhapsodic display of stringed instruments from the past 300 years.

To enhance your musical and museum experience, the exhibit is set inside the ancient church of San Maurizio, making it a purely exquisite experience!

Although old documents date the building back to 1088, its current Greek-Cross iteration was consecrated in 1828. Many of the decorative sculptures and paintings were done in the Classical Renaissance style.

The museum discusses the importance of instrument-making in Venice, most especially the violin. Venetian artisans became known throughout the musical world for their eye and ear toward perfection and quality.

A highlight is the artisan's room that was set up to look as though Geppetto would return to create new and perfect violins (rather than puppets).

This exhibit continues into the San Polo Sestiere inside the Church of San Giacomo di Rialto, where the Antonio Vivaldi 224 collection resides.

SAN MARCO

Sestiere

SAN MARCO

CHIESA di SANTO STEFANO

Founded in 1294, this church with the impressive interior was named after the Saints Augustine and Stefano by the Augustine Hermits of Sant'Anna. The exterior was designed with the plain Gothic style next to a cramped canal making photos difficult.

Inside, the soaring ship's keel roof is believed to have been created in the Arsenale by the ship-building experts. The nave and the walls have been patterned with diamonds and acanthus-leaves. Its columns alternate in red and white marble, accenting the checkerboard marble floor. Santo Stefano is populated with excellent Venetian art, including Tintoretto's "The Last Supper."

Santo Stefano has been rebuilt six times due to the massive bloodshed that had occurred within its walls over the centuries.

BULL FIGHTS
In the days of the Venetian Republic, bull fights were held in the Campo of Santo Stefano.

Sestiere

The Leaning Tower of Santo Stefano is a favorite site within the city. Read more about leaning towers 266.

RIALTO BRIDGE

SAN MARCO

*The Rialto Bridge is one of the most photographed, and certainly
one of the most loved bridges in the world.*

 The Rialto Bridge, or Ponte di Rialto, is one of the most stunning sites
you will see in Venice. For centuries, there was no way to cross the
Grand Canal on foot.

Way back in the Medieval times, the only way to cross the Grand Canal
was by a variety of boats and floating pontoons. During the 1100s (nearly
1,000 years ago!), demand for the need for a bridge became great enough
that the city decided to build a wooden bridge at this spot. This was the first
time people could cross the Grand Canal on foot!

The first bridge lasted some 70 years, when its collapse required it to be
replaced with another wooden bridge. Then during a revolt of the city in 1310
led by Bajamonte Tiepolo (not the artist, but an aristocratic predecessor),
the bridge was burned down, and was again replaced by another wooden
bridge. One hundred and fifty years later, this new bridge collapsed under the
weight of a crowd of people as they observed a boat parade in the water, and
was again replaced with yet another wooden bridge. Not to be undone, that
bridge collapsed swiftly in 1524.

In 1551, the city held a contest for someone to come up with a better idea for
the bridge. Many famous architects entered designs, including Michelangelo
and Palladio, but the job was given to Antonio da Ponte, who completed the
job in 1591.

The Renaissance-styled bridge was designed upon 12,000 pilings, with 2 inclined ramps and a high portico in the middle. Sceptics scoffed at this ludi-
crous design, but over 400 years later, the bridge stands today for your scenic
enjoyment.

Sestiere

FONDACO dei TEDESCHI

SAN MARCO

Ferragamo, Gucci, Versace, Moschino... and the list goes on. Tedeschi is an indoor shopping center for the big-name Italian and European designers. This grand old building has been converted into a grand new shopping mall, while maintaining its traditional Palladian-style interior architecture.

This mall has a secret that is a bit difficult to find. Within this splen-did shopping venue, is a red escalator that will take you up a few floors. When you get to the top floor, look around for a door with a staircase in it. Climb this last flight of stairs, and step out onto the roof of the building.

You will find yourself looking down over the Rialto Bridge, laid out amid one of the most spectacular views of the Grand Canal that is available to the public! Your time will be limited to just a few minutes, so hurry and take as many photos as you can. The view *(seen below)* is what you will have to look forward to. This treat is shockingly unknown to the general tourist crowd; so enjoy it before it catches on.

Sestiere

㊵ CASTELLO SESTIERE

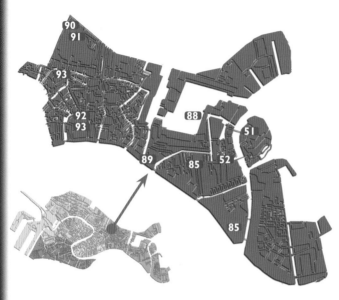

Castello is the largest of the six Sestiere in the city of Venice. Nearly half of Castello is occupied by the Arsenale, the Naval Base of Venice.

In the old days of the Republic, the Arsenale was the largest employer in the Serenissima, and the bulk of day workers lived here in Castello. Today, because of the Biennale **278** *(festival of art and architecture)*, Castello has a casual, artsy air. Via Garibaldi is a wide walk-street lined with local shops and restaurants. The quiet neighborhood and local eateries are a great way to meld with the locals and strike up a conversation. From the Garden, you can watch the boats pass by, and if a festival happens to be occurring, the Garden is a great place to observe. The Aqua Alta library is a local bookstore that barely endured a flood in its past. They recreated the store using the drenched books for climbable steps and other pieces of decor. The Scuola Grande San Marco (not to be confused with the Church of San Marco) is today a civil hospital with a fantastic Baroque architecture. Never will you see a hospital with this kind of elegant stature! Outside. you will find the statue of General Colleone created by the Renaissance master sculptor, Verrocchio. Some locals believe that because Verrocchio died before finishing the statue, that it was finished by his favorite student, a young Leonardo da Vinci. But alas, this wasn't so.

The skinniest street in Venice (or perhaps the world) Calletta Varisco is a tiny side street located near Campiello Stella.

Arsenale 88

This high-walled, Byzantine-styled structure was created during the 1100s as the heart of the Serenissima's ship-building power. At its peak, it employed 16,000 people who could produce one complete ship per day! This capability so out-weighed anyone else's that it enabled Venice to maintain a political, military, and economic power over the Western Mediterranean and Adriatic Seas.

Naval History Museum 89

The Museum was built just after WWI to fulfill a 200-year-old dream of the city. The exhibits inside tell the story of the rise and fall of the maritime power of the Serenissima. The Bucintoro (the Doge's ship), 256 shown here, is the highlight of the museum. The scale models of ancient ships are found all throughout.

Giardini della Bienale 85

In Venice, gardens are a rare thing indeed. The Biennale Gardens are often used for festivals, exhibits, performances, and picnics alike. During the Biennale, parts of the park offer exhibits and food stands alike. This is an excellent place to relax in the shade and leisurely watch the Venetian life pass you by.

Giuseppe Garibaldi 85

Garibaldi was a key proponent in the Unification of the existing city-states into a single unified Italy. This meant clearing the Austrians from the Venetian territories to free her from their rule. This statue of Garibaldi is a reminder of his significance to Venice and to Italy, as a whole.

CASTELLO

Siestiere

CASTELLO

Siestiere

90 Scuola Grande di San Marco

Sitting competitively adjacent to the massive Church of Sts. John & Paul is the Scuola di San Marco. Founded in 1260, this Classical Renaissance beauty boasted a long list of the Venetian elite as its members. The membership was so powerful that the Scuola Grande was able to assume the same name as the Patron Saint of the City.

91 Basilica dei Santi Giovanni e Paolo

This Venetian Gothic Parish Church, nicknamed "San Zanipolo" by the locals, was completed in the 1430s. It enjoys the status of a minor Basilica, here in the Castello Sestiere. This is where the funerals for all Doges were held, and there are 25 Doge tombs within its walls today. The church has three bells within its tower, all playing in D-Major.

91 Equestrian Statue of Bartolomeo Colleoni

Standing in the Campo outside of San Zanipolo and San Marco is the equestrian statue of Captain General Bartolomeo Colleoni. He left in his will that he would like a statue of himself to be placed in St Mark's Square. Because it is illegal to put non-religious idols in St. Mark's Square, 48 *they put it here, in front of St. Mark's Scuola Grande instead.*

92 Church of San Zaccaria

The orginal church on this site was built in the 800s to contain the remains of St. Zechariah, who was the father of John the Baptist. It was later rebuilt in the 1100s, then underwent a 50-year replacement starting in 1458. Additionally, this is the entry point to the underground catacombs of the Doges 93.

Catacombs of San Zaccaria 93

Upon entering the quiescent ambiance of the Church of San Zaccaria, a set of doors on the right will take you to a small, creepy staircase down into the bowels of the church. You will end up in the ancient crypts of eight long-dead Doges. Now flooded with water, it is roped off to prevent visitors from stepping into its murky waters. Visit it if you must!

Acqua Alta Bookstore 93

Since the construction, this building has consistently been inundated with high waters. So the owners decided to embrace it, instead of fight it. They have created an highly unusual retail store, cram-packed with books, magazines, maps, and other such bookish items. In the middle of the store is an authentic Gondola. This is a popular oddity for locals and visitors alike.

Ponte di Quintavalle - the Wooden Bridge 87

People commonly think that the Accademia Bridge is the only wooden bridge left in Venice. However, the wooden Ponte di Quintavalle is a great convenience for the locals. It connects Castello to the Island of San Pietro, and it also has one other point of convenience: unlike the 408 other bridges in Venice, this bridge has no stairs! Smooth rolling for wheelchairs, strollers, luggage, etc.

Veggie Boat 87

Where Via Girabaldi, the widest street in Castello, meets the canal, you will find the floating produce market. Take a break and purchase a healthy snack. Because shopping here is a local custom, this is a great place to strike up a conversation with the locals. You'll know that the fruits and veggies from this boat are of an exceptionally high quality.

CASTELLO

Siestiere

ARSENALE

CASTELLO

The Arsenale became
a world leader in the
manufacture of rope.

The Arsenale became so good at ship-building that
during the 1300s, it could produce one complete ship per day!

Siestiere

The Arsenale was originally built for the Republic of Venice in the 1100s, and was considered to be the world's largest pre-Industrial Revolution compound. It was responsible for the building of the Naval ships that gave Venice its power of the seas. Additionally, it produced all of the trading ships and transportation vessels for the Republic. It became the best place to maintain the ships as well.

In 1320, a new and improved Arsenale was built to up-size the original. Its ship-building prowess became so efficient that they could turn out one full ship per day! This single fact supported a sea-faring military and trading muscle that had never been seen before in the western world.

The Arsenale employed approximately 16,000 people during its height; most of whom lived in the nearby Castello Sestiere. They were specialists in every step of the building process: craftsmen to shape the wood, soakers to form it, tar-men to seal it, ropesmen, oarsmen, guys that supervised the bow, the stern, and midships. They operated a full assembly-line, many centuries before Henry Ford formalized the process, during the Industrial Revolution.

One of several ships' hangars in the Arsenale.

Munitions were also manufactured and stored here en masse.

By the mid-15th century, the Venetian fleet boasted over 3,000 ships: some for trading, some for transportation, and some for war. The ability to build such a massive fleet enabled Venice to maintain their front-row position as the Captains of Commerce for centuries.

The Naval ships would keep the trading ships safe during transport, as well as the forceful forging of new trade routes whenever they collided with other countries. The wealthy tradesmen and bankers got wealthier. They in turn invested in the high-cost of maintaining the enormous fleet, thereby solidifying their expanding positions as the Captains of Commerce. The possession of such a mechanism made Venice the strongest military and trading power the Western World had ever seen at that point in history.

All of this power stemmed from the Venice Arsenale.

NAVAL HISTORY MUSEUM

The Navy Museum tells the stories of the impressive array of wartime vessels that were created within the confines of the Arsenale. With over 25,000 pieces exhibited, the Museum covers Venetian Maritime history going back to the 12th century.

Shown here is the most famous Bucintoro **256**, the galley used by the Doge to perform the "Marriage at Sea" ceremony each year, during the Festa della Sensa.

Besides traditional warships, centuries of Gondolas are displayed demonstrating their local evolution.

CASTELLO

Siestiere

SAN MARCO
Scuola Grande

Sitting competitively adjacent to the massive Church of Sts. John & Paul is the Scuola di San Marco. Founded in 1260, this Classical Renaissance beauty boasted a long list of the Venetian elites as its members. The membership was so powerful that the Scuola Grande was able to assume the same name as the Patron Saint of the City.

It's function as a Scuola ended when Napoleon ended the Venetian Republic in 1797. Later under the Austrian rule, it was used as a military hospital. Today it functions as a city hospital.

The decoration of the Scuola was completed under the grand triumvirate by the world renowned Renaissance master Jacopo Tintoretto: "The Miracle of the Slave" **139**, "Finding St. Mark's Body," and "Stealing the Body of Saint Mark" **217**. "Finding" is now hanging in the Pinacoteca di Brera in Milan, and the other two can be enjoyed in the Gallerie dell'Accademia in Venice.

QUEST ITEM
Can you find this Little Red Heart? It is hiding inside Sotoportego dei Preti in the Castello Sestiere. We don't know anything about it, but it was unique enough to cause curiosity.

Church of Sts. JOHN & PAUL
Chiesa dei San Giovanni e San Paolo

This Venetian Gothic Parish Church was completed in the 1430s, and enjoys the status of a minor Basilica, here in the Castello Sestiere. This is where the funerals for all Doges were held, and there are 25 Doge tombs within its walls today. The church has three bells within its tower, all playing in D-Major.

Inside is a harmonious assemblage of Venetian artworks, created by the most ebullient artists in Venice. Included is the ethereal "Annunciation" by Veronese, a trompe l'oeil *(trick of the eye)* that erupts through the ceiling and proceeds into the heavens.

The most notable artists include: Giovanni Bellini, Veronese, Lombardo, Bartolomeo Bon, and Vivarini.

Tombs of the most notable Doges include: Jacopo & Lorenzo Tiepolo, Giovanni & Alviso I Mocenigo, Morosini, and Vendremin.

• •

Standing proudly in the Campo outside of Scuola San Marco is the equestrian statue of Captain Gen. Bartolomeo Colleoni. He stated in his will that he would like a statue of himself to be placed in Saint Mark's Square 48 . The

problem is that Saint Mark's Square can have only religious icons - not military statues - displayed. So to appease his descendants, the city placed this statue in front of St. Mark's Scuola instead of St. Mark's Square.

It is noteworthy because the statue was created by the early Florentine Renaissance master Andrea del Verrocchio. Verrocchio was the teacher of such greats as Leonardo da Vinci 129 , among many others. Point in fact: as a young student, Leonardo da Vinci himself had a hand in creating this monument as well. Verrocchio died before seeing the completion of this statue, and so it was completed by Alessandro Leopardi.

Chiesa di SAN ZACCARIA

The original church on this site was built in the 800s to contain the remains of St. Zechariah, the father of John the Baptist. It was later rebuilt in the 1100s, then underwent a 50-year replacement starting in 1458. The replacement began with a Gothic design, when a number of designers stepped in, and was later finished in an early-renaissance style by Mauro Codussi. This structure has a similar profile to the Chiesa di Santa Maria Novella in Florence.

In the below-ground catacombs are the Doge's crypts. They can be entered through the main church with a small admittance fee that will let you go down to see the tombs.

Its Convent was considered to be the most important female religious institute in Venice. Way back in 864, the headpiece of the Doge was donated by the Nuns of the Convent. Additionally, they donated the land needed for the expansion of Saint Mark's Square. Each year on Easter, the Doge 59 begins a Procession at San Zaccaria involving the donning of the Doge's cap in thanks for their graciousness.

For years, the Convent was a place for the wealthy families to keep their daughters until marriage. This had to do with the assurance of chastity, in order to inherit the family's wealth. The Nuns were known for their relaxed notions of the Convent rules.

QUEST ITEM

Can you find this Gargoyle? It was not placed on the outside of the Church of Santa Maria Formosa to scare you away. It was put there to protect the locals by scaring away the evil spirits. He's a fun selfie buddy!

Inside San Zaccaria, you will still find the tomb of Saint Zechariah near the altar. The artwork around the walls are stunning and observance should be taken slowly. Existing are pieces from a wide variety of famous artists, including pieces from Bellini, Tiepolo, Titian, and the Dutchman, van Dyck.

CATACOMBS of S. ZACCARIA

Upon entering the quiescent ambiance of the Church of San Zaccaria, a set of doors on the right will take you to a small creepy staircase down into the bowels of the church. You will end up in the ancient crypts of eight long-dead Doges. The eerie atmosphere is exactly as it would be in an old fright-night movie. Now flooded with water, it is roped off to prevent visitors from falling into its murky waters.

ACQUA ALTA BOOK STORE

In Venice, Acqua Alta *(High Waters)* are common. In fact, in 1966, the city saw over 1-meter of flooding of briny lagoon waters. This is often pointed to as proof that the island is sinking. During the 20th century, Venice has measured only 10 centimeters (3.9") of reduced altitude.

Regularly, visitors will notice a splashing over the walls or seepage coming up through the grounds of Saint Mark's Square. This typically occurs during the high tides of a full moon and during unusually bad winters.

The reduction in altitude happened in the first part of the 20th century because of geological issues and a natural compression of the wooden pilings underneath the city.

The larger issue is the rising of the sea levels. Many ideas are in place to help stem off this potentially oncoming problem for Venice, such as the MOSE project which is building underwater floodgates to prevent large-scale flooding over time.

One such victim of constant high waters is the Libreria Acqua Alta, the High Water Book Store. Since its construction, it has consistently been inundated with high waters. With the drowned volumes, they created a unusual retail store cram-packed with books, magazines, maps, and other such bookish items. In the middle of the store, is an authentic Gondola 252, also overloaded with books. It has become a neighborhood favorite and a gotta-see oddity while you are in Castello.

CANNAREGIO SESTIERE

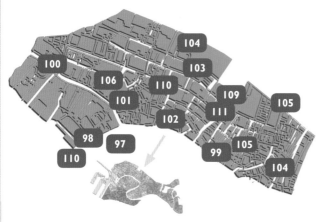

The calmness of Cannaregio (the top of the fish, **27**) provides a much-needed respite from the other tourist-driven Sestiere of Venice. With a history steeped in drama, it is now the most desirable neighborhood for the locals. It is doused with eateries where the locals casually enjoy their own cultural Venetian food and sense of humor. Taking the time to stroll off the main streets will reward you with a way to get a deeper understanding of how the locals live. Don't be shy about entering their cafes. As long as your manners are good, you will be welcomed - just as you would have it when strangers enter your own local haunts.

Stroll down the wide Strada Nova, which will take you from the Guglie Bridge to the Rialto Bridge. Leave the main strada to find some of these wonderful surprises all along the way: fewer tourists, more local eateries, churches, bars, and an endless number of local ciccheterias (appetizer bars) will be yours to enjoy.

As you stroll northward off the Fonda-mente Nove, you will find smaller streets lined with local cafes. Do not hesitate to try them. These are great places to take in the local sites, while taking a few selfies.

98 Santa Lucia/Ferrovia Train Station

The Church of Santa Lucia was demol-ished by the Austrians in 1861. This was done to make room for both the trains themselves as well as the station building.

Ca' D'oro 99

(Palazzo Santa Sofia)

Completed in 1430 for the Contarini family, today it displays the donated collection of Giorgio Franchetti. The floor, which you see here, was painstakingly decorated, cut stone by cut stone to create this stunning room. Walk across it for a peek out the window to the stunning Grand Canal below.

Ponte dei Tre Archi 100

The only triple-arched bridge remaining in Venice, it was built by Andrea Tirali in 1681. This bridge is on the last leg of the world-famous Gondola Race known as La Vogalonga 274 *, making this an excellent spot from which to view the contenders.*

Ponte della Guglie 101

Known also as the Bridge of Spires for the 4 obelisks standing tall at the ends of the bridge, it was originally made from wood in 1285, recreated in stone in 1581 by Contarini, then rebuilt two more times over the next centuries. The Guglie bridge connects the Strada Nova to the Santa Lucia train station.

Casinò/Wagner Museum 102

Housed in a grand Renaissance palace, Ca' Vendramin Calergi, Venice's casinò is always keen to attract tourists, offering a free boat shuttle from Piazzale Roma and free entrance with a special leaflet (look at the tourist office or in your hotel). The famous German composer Richard Wagner died in the building: his room can be visited with a previously-set appointment.

CANNAREGIO

Sestiere

CANNAREGIO

Sestiere

103 Tintoretto's House
On the Fondamenta dei Mori is the house where Tintoretto, one of the most famous artists in the world, spent his life. A quick stroll around the corner is the church of the Madonna dell'Orto; otherwise known as the Church of Tintoretto due to the huge amount of works created by him within.

103 Campo dei Mori
Three brothers, Sandi, Afani and Rioba Mastelli from Greece (Morea), were traders of spices and silks. They had earned a reputation for their harsh business tactics. Local legend has it that Maria Magdellena turned them to stone in payment for their greed. You will find all three brothers here.

104 Santa Maria dei Miracoli
On the east side of Canareggio is a marble gem of a Renaissance church. Built in the 1480s by Pietro Lombardo, it gave a home for the miraculous statue of the Virgin Mary. It is known by the locals to be the prettiest church in Venice for weddings.

104 Madonna dell'Orto - the church of Tintoretto
Right around the corner from Tintoretto's house lies the church which he attended all of his life. To show his dedication, he spent years of his adult life creating a massive number of pieces that are still on display in their original context in this beautiful little church.

105 Fondamente Nove & Strada Nova
A stroll along these streets will give you views of the lagoon, as well as a way to pass through the entire Sestiere of Cannaregio. Combined, these streets (and their side streets) will give you a great feel for the locally-inhabited Cannaregio.

Jewish Ghetto

During the mid 1500s on this section of Cannaregio, an old Foundry was closed down and cleared out. The area where they used to pile their leavings was called a Geto. (The origin of the word 'Ghetto' is still in dispute, even today.)

Scuola Grande di Santa Maria della Misericordia

The Scuola di Santa Maria della Misericordia is recognized as one of the original seven Scuola Grandi **29** *of Venice. Building began in 1308 in the strong Gothic style.*

Old Teatro Grocery Store

As you can see by the signage, this fabulous old building used to be a theatre for the residents of Cannaregio, and it still looks like one. Walk inside and you will be hit with a modern-day grocery store; complete with displays up on the loges.

Ponte della Costituzione **110**

This bridge connects the main transportation hubs on the Tronchetto **167**. *It joins the Santa Lucia train station on Cannaregio to the bus station and the main boat dock on Santa Croce. Opened in 2008, it is the newest bridge in Venice.*

Ponte degli Scalzi **97**

One of only four bridges that stretch over the Grand Canal, the Scalzi Bridge connects the train station on Cannaregio to the San Polo Sestiere. A long bridge, it makes for a wonderful place to watch the water vessels pass underneath.

The Bridge with no Handrails **111**

If you are curious to know what many of the bridges looked like a thousand years ago, Ponte di Chiodo is a good example. Once, many bridges looked like this, but today there are only two left in the entire city. Also note that it leads to a private residence rather than to another street.

CANNAREGIO

Sestiere

CANNAREGIO

Sestiere

SANTA LUCIA TRAIN STATION
Ferrovia

In the spot where the train station sits, a church once stood in its place. The Church of Santa Lucia and her Convent were destroyed in 1861, while Venice was still under Austrian Rule.

In the photo to the right, the left side of the Liberty Bridge was the original train bridge that the Austrians built in the 19th century. The automobile lanes were added much later in the 20th century. Today, all vehicles find their way to Venice and do not go further then the edge of the island. Because the island consists of over 400 foot-bridges, no vehicles of any sort are allowed to go past the initial parking lot.

Arrivals and departures to/ from the train station are made simple. The Vaporetto *(water bus)* stops at the Fer- rovia stop directly in front of the station.

The modern Costituzione bridge **110** will take you to the bus station and to the car lots on the Tronchetto **167**.

QUEST ITEM

This little Winged Lion is waiting near the corner of a bar in Cannaregio. Can you find it? Ask a local if you get stuck!

CA' D'ORO

Ca' d'Oro, or Golden House, was aptly named when its edges and trimmings were decorated with a gold gilting. Technically called Palazzo Santa Sofia, this floral Baroque beauty set on the Grand Canal is a visitor's photo favorite. Her gallery boasts famous Venetian artists such as Tintoretto, Tiepolo, and Carpaccio. Additionally, works from the Dutch artists Van Dyck and Van Eyck are present. Many of the items in Ca' d'Oro were torn from Venetian churches during the takeover of Napoleon. These would include a sumptuous variety of paintings, sculptures, bronzes, and tapestries. Ca' Duodo next door contains an assortment of ceramics that have been rescued from all around the Venetian Lagoon.

Ca' d'Oro was built for the Contarini family by Bartolomeo and Giovanni Bon. Similar in design to the Doge's Palace, Ca' d'Oro has three levels: the loggia and the two higher floors. The quatrefoils (4-sided architectural trimmings) line the top of the middle balcony, and pointed arches were used for both upper levels. The close columns lend to stunning views of the Grand Canal from inside the building looking out.

This high relief sculpture of the Last Supper is reminiscent of da Vinci's painting; because the artist, Tullio Lombardo, wanted to show his love for Leonardo's work. Ca' d'Oro displays exceptional collections of paintings, sculptures, and tapestries - mostly, but not entirely - from famous Venetian artists.

Giorgio Franchetti created this magnificent 350 sq-meter floor in the loggia of Ca' d'Oro. His love and dedication to the house resonated in this, his life's project. Unfortunately, he died before he got to show it off. The marble pieces of this colorful mosaic were gathered from all over Italy. He spent years hand-cutting and laying this floor. When you come to Venice, it would be a shame to miss this extravagant work of love and beauty.

CANNAREGIO

Sestiere

TRE ARCHI BRIDGE
(3 Arches Bridge)

CANNAREGIO

Sestiere

On the north end of the Canale di Cannaregio is the Tre Archi Bridge. Andrea Tirali built this Baroque-styled bridge in 1681. The last of the triple-arched bridges left in Venice, it features several coats-of-arms left from wealthy residents of centuries past. The two empty niches pose somewhat of a mystery, as it is not known why Tirali put them there. It seems they should each hold a beautiful statue or some such local monument. No historical documents, drawings, nor paintings show these spaces filled with anything. It seems to be an opportunity for a sculptor of the future!

QUEST ITEM

Can you find the Camel? It is in plain sight if you are visiting the area of Tintoretto's house. It is on the wall of Palazzo Mastelli across from Campo dei Mori.

GUGLIE BRIDGE

Stretching across the Canale di Cannaregio is the picturesque Ponte delle Guglie, or the Guglie Bridge, or Bridge of Spires. It was originally built from wood, but was later replaced in 1580 with the stone bridge you see

"Gargoyles" across the face of the Guglie

today. It was restored nearly every century, and during its rebuild in 1823, the four obelisks were added. In 1987, the city added a wheelchair access, stone steps, and a metal handrail.

Near the east end of the bridge is a small doorway leading to the Jewish Ghetto, just north of the bridge. The Guglie is a wonderful spot for the perfect Venetian selfie!

Did You Know...

The Margherita Pizza was named after Margherita, the Queen of Italy, (1878) who was loved more than her husband or their son. The ingredients represent the colors in the Italian flag: Basil, Mozzarella Cheese, and Tomato. The popular Caprese salad carries these colors as well.

CASINÒ di Venezia/WAGNER Museu

Housed in a grand Renaissance palace of Ca' Vendramin Calergi, Venice's casino is always keen to attract tourists, offering a free boat shuttle from Piazzale Roma and free entrance with a special leaflet *(check the tourist office or in your hotel)*. Many people have owned the house over the centuries, but it is most known for the fact that the famous German Composer Richard Wagner **233** died during his stay in the building: his rooms can be visited at pre-scheduled times.

Construction began in 1481 by Mauro Codussi, the same architect of the Church of San Zaccaria, as well as other churches and homes in Venice. It took 26 years to complete, due to his death before its completion. However, because of the technology of the day, taking 26 years to complete a building was more common than not.

QUEST ITEM
Cannaregio is fun to visit, as you will find the delightful personality of the locals all throughout the neighborhood. Can you find this humorous door? It is hiding in plain sight in Cannaregio, near to a Bridge of Fists.

TINTORETTO'S HOUSE

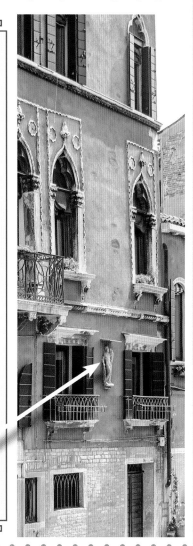

Tintoretto and the Witch

Local legend tells that Tintoretto's daughter, Marietta, on her way to the church one morning, was met by a witch. This woman gave her a bag of Communal Host (bread) and told her to eat one every day. In doing so, she would eventually become Saintly and Madonna-like, but it would only happen if she kept this a secret. Marietta, a clever girl, buried the bread in her garden every day, instead of eating them. Eventually, Marietta told her father, Tintoretto, of the old lady, the bread, and the promise. Realizing that this was the trick of a witch, Tintoretto asked Marietta to invite the old lady for a visit. Hiding behind the door, Tintoretto clubbed the old lady on the head. Letting out a harsh scream, the witch vanished in a cloud of smoke and streamed out of the building through a hole in the wall. Today you will see a high-relief of Hercules holding a club outside of Tintoretto's house. It is said that he put it there to cover that hole in the wall and to scare the witch into never returning, with the threat of the club.

CAMPO dei MORI

Next to Tintoretto's house is the little Campo dei Mori. Three Moorish brothers *("Mori")*, who were instrumental in assisting Doge Dandolo in the Sacking of Constantinople, can be found here. Because of their greedy ways, Mary Magdeline turned them into stone, to remind the locals that greed will not end well.

CANNAREGIO

Sestiere

SANTA MARIA dei MIRACOLI

On the east side of Canareggio is a marble gem of a Renaissance church. Built in the 1480's by Pietro Lombardo, it gave a home for the miraculous statue of the Virgin Mary. It is known by the locals to be the prettiest church for Weddings in Venice.

MADONNA del ORTO

The church was named for a statue of the Virgin Mary that was found in a nearby orchard. Once she found her home here, it provided the perfect name of Santa Maria Madonna del Orto (orchard).

This is the church in which the famous Renaissance master, Tintoretto, grew up. He lived around the corner and ran here every day for mass. As an adult, he came here daily to give thanks by creating a large cache of paintings for the church. Each of the chapels is beautifully decorated with his work. So much did he love this church, above all others, that he wished to be entombed here.

FONDAMENTE NOVE

Cannaregio is one of the best places to simply stroll, as it includes these two long wide streets where you will not get lost.

A waterfront stroll along the Fondamente Nove will give you views of the Lagoon, of Isla San Michele (the mortuary island) and Murano (the glass island) across the water. You can board the Vaporetto here to visit the islands of Murano, Burano, and Torcello. A relaxed seafood dinner can be found along the waterfront, as well as a cool gelato and a stunning view!

STRADA NOVA

Strada Nova is a great place to stroll with a gelato in your hand. This wide street will take you from the Rialto Bridge through Cannaregio, all the way to the Santa Lucia Train Station!

Shops, restaurants, and churches line the sides of this street. You will pass great places like Ca'D'Oro, the Casino, and the Richard Wagner Museum.

Along the way, try to find the old Theater that is now a grocery market; then rest on the Guglie Bridge for the view.

CANNAREGIO

Sestiere

CANNAREGIO

JEWISH GHETTO

During the mid-1500s in this section of Cannaregio, an old copper foundry was closed down and cleared out. The area where they used to pile their leavings was called a Geto. *(The origin of the word 'Ghetto' is still in dispute, even today.* 108 *)*

This land was developed with housing for the Jews to both segregate, as well as for their own protection. The neighborhood is divided into the New Ghetto and the Old Ghetto, but this is misleading because these names were related to their usage back when it was a Foundry. The initial part of the Jewish Ghetto was built on the 'new' Foundry area, and the new extensions, that were later added to the Jewish neighborhood, was built on the 'old' foundry area. Confusing, I know.

The Ghetto was surrounded by a wall, with an entrance bridge on two opposite sides. Each night, a gate was locked to block the crossing of the bridges. This area was well guarded, with limited hours of entry and exit, but people were free to come and go as they pleased, so long as they returned home before the gates were locked each evening. The Venetians felt this was for the safety of the Jews. Additionally, the Jews were free to build Synagogues and practice their own faith.

In the Vatican-influenced Venice, Catholics were not allowed to lend money. This opened the door for the Jewish community to become the lenders of the City, making this neighborhood into a profitable financial hub. This was good for the Venetians because it meant they didn't have to go to the mainland to get and pay their loans. The Venetians enjoyed this relationship so much that they provided protection for the Jews against raiders, robbers, war, etc.

The Ghetto was not designated as a 'poor' neighborhood, but more of a segregated neighborhood. Somehow, the word Ghetto has come to mean a poor, under-managed, under-privileged neighborhood. When Napoleon took over in 1797, he opened the doors to the neighborhood, thereby

Sestiere

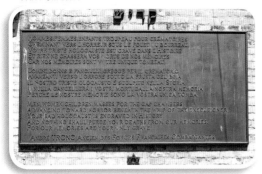

A series of memorial plaques remain on the walls in the Jewish Ghetto, a reminder to the Venetians of the tragic loss of so many of their Jewish friends. In 1938, fascist racial laws deprived the Jews of civil rights and the Nazi persecutions began. Two hundred and forty six Jews were deported from Venice; only eight returned from the death camps.

ending Jewish segregation forever. As the population within the walls of the Ghetto grew, the city gave permission to build taller buildings than the rest of Venice. Additionally, it was approved to create substandard-height ceilings to squeeze more floors into those taller buildings. Today this neighborhood is an open lively part of Venice, where five Synagogues still exist that have represented the three ethnic groups that came to Venice from all around Europe. The Jewish Information Center will provide much history of the area, and a must-see is the nicely-done Museo Ebraico which will give an in-depth accounting of the lifestyle of the Venetian Jews.

In Venice, it was illegal for Catholics to lend money. What a perfect niche for the Jews because it saved the Venetians from having to go to the mainland each time they had to make a loan payment. Banco Rosso gave a red-colored receipt each time a person pawned an item in exchange for money, making it easy for the borrower to remember he had a debt to pay. This is how the term **'in the red'** became synonymous with being in debt. Banco Rosso is open today for visitation.

CANNAREGIO

Sestiere

Jewish Ghetto

CANNAREGIO

Sestiere

In 1516, the Venetian Senate ruled that the Jews in Venice must move to a section of the island called the "Ghetto." This decision was to prevent further ongoing skirmishes between the local Christians and the growing Jewish population.

The ruling to segregate them was considered to be a positive step toward the Jews, as it provided a sanctuary for them to practice their religion, without further issues from the Christians. Even though their new community was gated, the residents were free to come and go as they pleased on a daily basis.

When inside their boundaries, they lived an ordinary life. The Venetians did invoke a curfew upon them stating that Ghetto residents must be back inside the gates by midnight or they would be locked out. There were, however, two exceptions to this rule: medical professionals and musicians.

As the population grew, the boundaries did not. So the Jews decided to build upwards; the Ghetto has the

The Word "Ghetto"

In the Ghetto area of Venice, there once stood an old copper refinery. Its refuse area was called a Geto, an Italian word. It was simply an old industrial carry-over word. It has since been 'Venetian-ized' into the word Ghetto that we know today, and has since evolved into a negative term.

tallest buildings in Venice - not counting the churches, of course.

When Napoleon came along in 1797, he had the gates to the Jewish Ghetto removed, but the local Jews preferred their neighborhood to that of the outside Venetian community, so the ridding of the barriers did not invoke much change in their behavior at that point.

Today more than 100,000 tourists visit the Ghetto each year. The five original synagogues created for the various populations of Jews are still standing and open to visitors: the Spanish, the Levantine, the Canton, the Great German, and the Italian Scuolas.

MISERICORDIA
Scuola Grande

The Scuola di Santa Maria della Misericordia, is recognized as one of the original seven Scuola Grandi of Venice. Building began in 1308 in the strong Gothic style. Jacopo Sansovino, the famous Florentine architect, arrived in Venice to design the 'New Scuola.' Using his taste and skills for Classical design, he created a stunning Roman interior while staying loyal to the traditional Gothic exterior and layout.

The interior is decorated with artworks for some of the most famous Venetian artists such as Domenico Tintoretto (son of the famous Jacopo Tintoretto), Veronese, and Pelligrini. Included are drawings by Palladio depicting the early building.

Misericordia has been transformed over the centuries with several wholly different uses. In 1806, Napoleon used it for military purposes. In 1815, it was used to warehouse liquids. The year 1831 saw it turn into a hospital. In 1914, it became a Sports Club, where the sport of Basketball became quite famous in Venice. In 2016, it saw the completion of yet another restoration and was inaugurated as the Scuola Grande della Misericordia, now a gallery of fine art.

Visitors today will enjoy a wide variety of art and historical exhibits in this many-storied building.

EX-THEATRE/GROCERY STORE

Have you ever shopped for groceries in a building with ceilings like this? What about one with theatre balconies, Renaissance style? Once an ancient theatre, it is now occupied by a grocery store. Although we tried, we couldn't find any popcorn, however. A bit hard to find because the store sits in a corner, humbly disguised as an old theatre. Just ask the locals because this is a sweet treat!

Ponte della COSTITUZIONE

Sestiere

This bridge, named PONTE CALATRAVA for its architect, connects the main transportation hubs of Tronchetto. It joins the Santa Lucia train station on Cannaregio to the bus station and to the main Vaporetto boat dock on San Polo. Opened in 2008, it is the newest bridge in Venice. It's name celebrates the 60th birthday of the Italian Constitution. The sight of a 21st century bridge looks out of place, within this city of antiquities. But fear not: in another 1,000 years, it will look as ancient as everything else!

BRIDGE with No HANDRAILS

If you are curious to know what many of the bridges looked like 1,000 years ago, Ponte di Chiodo is a good example. Once, many bridges looked like this, but today, out of 403 bridges, there are only two left in the entire city that have no handrails. Also note: it leads to a private residence rather than to another street, which is an unusual privilege in Venice. If you can find this little treasure, keep your balance!

CITY PARKS

There are only a few green spots in Venice. Most old cities have long since been over-taken by the needs of man, and few have green areas left. Venice has three or four parks in the city: Parco Savorgnan (pictured here), Giardini Papado-poli, and Giardini della Biennale, plus a couple of smaller green areas. Parco Savorgnan in Cannaregio is great for families, picnics, and quiet cool moments under the trees.

CANNAREGIO

Sestiere

80 SAN POLO SESTIERE

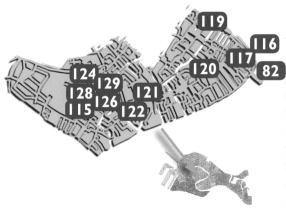

The smallest of the six Sestiere, San Polo has its own unique personality. Crossing the famous and picturesque Rialto Bridge enables you to see two Sestieres: San Polo on the north side and San Marco Sestiere on the south side. Like the other Sestiere, San Polo has a main street that is lined with gift shops and restaurants. At the Rialto Bridge end, it is called the Ruga Vecchia San Giovanni. It is a lovely way to stroll through San Polo - without getting lost. Near the Rialto Bridge, you will come to the famous Rialto Fish Market. You must get their early in the day, because it closes around 2 p.m. The further you walk away from the Rialto Bridge, the more authentic the shops and the restaurants become. As you pass through the small Campo Sant'Aponal, take a peek into the Church. Closed to religious ceremonies and stripped of its artworks in 1810, it has been used as a mill and grain storage facility, as well as a temporary prison to house people who were detained during Austrian control. This is a local neighbourhood, with a consistent stream of tourists passing through on the main path. (Notice that the main path has now changed names to Calle del Todeschini. Don't get used to it because the further you walk, the more names it will become!) Further along the path, you will come to the 2nd largest Campo in Venice, San Polo. *(Saint Mark's Square is the largest.)* Again, a local Campo and a great place to get a gelato and watch the locals go about their day. The Church of San Polo is a striking example of Gothic architecture. As you walk around it, notice the two 12th century lions guarding the base of the bell tower.

Most tourists never leave the San Marco Sestiere, so if you have come to San Polo: then we know you are an explorer. Here in San Polo, take note of little bridges with empty Gondolas 252 parked near them - the Gondolier won't be far away. Here you might find a fair price, and often, without lines.

Rialto Bridge

There are four bridges spanning the Grand Canal - the Rialto being the oldest of them. Constructed in the 12th century as a wooden pontoon bridge, it has suffered a tortured history. It collapsed several times under the weight of its crowds and burned during a revolt. Today, with its myriad of art and jewelry shops, it serves as one of the most recognizable tourist attractions in the city.

Campo Erberia

This is a favorite place for so many reasons. It is located between the Rialto Bridge (you can see the bridge between the buildings) and the Rialto Mercado - the daily fresh fish market. This photo was taken during a quiet morning, but as the day moves forward, this little Campo bustles with life and food and spirits.

Chiesa di San Giacomo di Rialto

According to local legend, this church was consecrated in 421ce making it the oldest church in the city. The 15th century clock, although picturesque, is the brunt of local jokes because it "maintains true inaccuracy." It is said that to mark the beginning of the city, the first brick was laid in this church. The pavement was raised to stave off the rising waters.

Rialto Fish Mercato

A popular place for both locals and tourists is the Rialto Fish Market. It opens around 3 a.m. to provide the freshest of seafood and farm goods to the local restaurants. It closes around 2 p.m., so be sure to get there early if you are planning a picnic. The butcheries display beautiful cuts of meat, and farmers hawk their fruits & veggies that had been cut fresh from the vine.

SAN POLO

Sestiere

SAN POLO

Sestiere

120 Sant'Aponal

Sant'Aponal is a local Campo with two areas: on one side, a constant stream of tourists pass through as they follow the main path. On the other, the locals hang out by the well in the middle, watching the tourists go by. A single restaurant serves all. [PLEASE: Tell the restaurateur Francesco that your friend Patty says 'Hi'!] 😜

121 Campo & Chiesa San Polo

The 2nd largest Campo behind San Marco, it is usually populated with local children playing ball. The main path runs through it giving tourists a glimpse into daily Venetian life.

122 Carlo Goldoni's House

The plays that brought comedy and sass to the stage made Carlo Goldoni as cherished in Venice as Shakespeare was in England. This former home of Goldoni is now a museum of theatrical study. On display are a variety of his personal effects, a collection of his writings, as well as an assortment of Venetian theatrical artifacts.

124 Scuola Grande di San Rocco

Saint Rock is the patron saint of plagues and of dogs (especially those bringing bread). Tintoretto fans: feast your tired eyes on the sheer amount of artistic force that is present in this building. The Annunciation, Adoration of the Magi, Flight to Egypt, Pillar of Fire, and the Adoration of the Shepherd, are but a few of the pieces from this Venetian Renaissance grand Maestro.

SAN POLO

Sestiere

Assassin's Creed®2 ~ The Video Game
San Polo was used as a principal backdrop for the video game Assassin's Creed®2. Noticeable in the game are San Rocco, Santa Maria Glorioso dei Frari, and the Rialto Bridge, among others. In the game, the two Sestieri of San Polo and Santa Croce were blended into one single area.

Santa Maria Gloriosa dei Frari 126

A Franciscan Basilica, created with the Venetian Gothic style, it houses an immense body of great works: including Bellini's famous Frari Triptych altarpiece. Donatello's St. John the Baptist, Sansovino's St. John the Baptist, and pieces by Sansovino, Veneziano, and Titian, three of Venice's favorite Renaissance greats.

Scuola Grande San Giovanni Evangelista di Venezia 128

Built by a confraternity of flagellants in 1261, it is believed that the success and wealth of this Scuola is due to the fact that it houses a true relic of the Cross given to them by the Chancellor of the Kingdom of Jerusalem. It became a Scuola Grande under the control of the "Council of Ten" during the Renaissance period.

Palazetto Bru Zane 115

This small theatre is dedicated to the love of French Romantic music. They hold regular chamber-sized performances and boast a wonderful collection of cd's and books for purchase. Take one of their scheduled tours to see the inside of this delightful surprise. If you wish to unwind and dream during your trip in Venice, this little gem is a must-do for you.

Museo Leonardo da Vinci 129

Although Leonardo didn't live in Venice, he did visit during his lifetime. While a young student, he worked on the bronze statue of General Bartolomeo Colleone which stands outside of the Scuola Grande de San Marco in Castello. Besides his famous artworks, da Vinci is also remembered as a highly creative engineer.

CAMPO ERBERIA

Located between the Rialto Bridge (you can see the bridge between the buildings) and the Rialto Mercado - the daily fresh fish market, this area is popular for lunch, appetizers (cicchetti), and dinner. This photo was taken during a quiet morning, but as the day moves forward, this little Campo bustles with life and food and spirits. This is one of many gondola 'parking lots' and when they are away, you can sit on the edge, dangle your feet over the side, and enjoy an Aperol Spritz. The view across the Grand Canal (below) is lined with ancient palazzos and fantastic architecture. The Vaporetto's will pass, the gondolas will idle by, and the water taxis will zip through this curve, all while you enjoy a gelato!

SAN GIACOMO di RIALTO

According to local legend, this church was consecrated in 421ce, making it the oldest church in the city. It is said that to mark the beginning of the city, the first brick was laid in this church. It was originally built as a gift to San Giacomo for saving the church when a disastrous fire broke out and burned everything in Rialto, except in this immediate area. The 15th-century clock, although picturesque, is the brunt of local jokes because as they say, it "maintains true inaccuracy." The pavement was raised to stave off the rising waters. While you are here, don't forget to fill your water bottle with the clean water of the well. Everyone does it, visitors and locals alike. It is surprisingly refreshing and cold!

QUEST ITEM

The Gobbo di Rialto (the Hunchback) is somewhere near the fountain (left).

This is where important notices were read during ancient times. Can you find him? If you get lost, simply ask a local.

SAN POLO

Sestiere

Is It Done Yet?

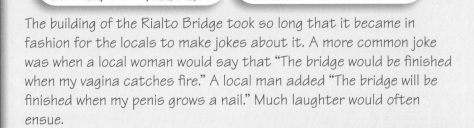

The building of the Rialto Bridge took so long that it became in fashion for the locals to make jokes about it. A more common joke was when a local woman would say that "The bridge would be finished when my vagina catches fire." A local man added "The bridge will be finished when my penis grows a nail." Much laughter would often ensue.

This joke became so popular amongst the locals that when they constructed the building *(top photo)* adjacent to the Rialto Bridge, they included these two high reliefs: on the left, a man with a finger nail for a penis, and a woman with her vagina on fire. *(What can I say? This is 500 year-old translated humor!)*

NOTE: to find the reliefs, climb several steps up the north side of the bridge Rialto Bridge and look back at the Camerlenghi building adjacent. They shouldn't be difficult to find.

MERCATO di RIALTO

A popular place for locals and tourists alike is the Rialto Fish Market. It opens around 3:00 a.m. to provide the freshest of seafood and farm goods to the local restaurants. It closes at 2:00 p.m., so be sure to get there early if you are planning a wonderful meal in your room. In the photo above, the mercato is in the open tarp-covered area as well as in the big building with the arches in the foreground. The market is divided into 2 areas: the Pescaria where fish is sold, and the Erberia where fresh produce is sold. The butcheries display beautiful cuts of fresh meats, and the farmers are hawking their fruits and veggies, cut fresh from the vine.

The most important food in Venice is the seafood. The fishermen arrive to schlep the fish, the shell fish, the clawed and the tentacled to appease the huge variety of local restaurants and chefs throughout the city. Tourists love to snap photos of the variety and the ambience. Surrounding the fish market are an abundance of umbrellaed vendors selling Venetian trinkets of every sort.

SANT'APONAL

The Gothic church in Campo Sant'Aponal was built in the 11th century and dedicated to Saint Apollonaire, the patron saint of Good Teeth. It was de-consecrated and had been used as a prison for political prisoners. Today it is merely an archive.

Rumor has it that Pope Alexander III hid in this church while hiding out from Barbarossa, the guy that wanted to steal his Pope-ship from him during one of the great Schisms.

Sant'Aponal has a local Campo with two areas: on one side a stream of tourists pass through, as they follow the main path. On the other, the locals hang out by the well. A single restaurant serves all. *[PLEASE: Tell the restaurateur Francesco that your friend Patty says 'Hi'!]*

The local feel of Sant'Aponal will strike you immediately, as it is not teeming with tourists - except those on the yellow path - but with every kind of local. And friendly they are! Take a bit of time to stop for a gelato or a Spritz, sit back and enjoy the local neighborhood.

CHIESA di SAN POLO

This Gothic structure was built in the 1400's although another church stood in this place since the late 800's. The ceiling has a high-reaching ship's keel design laying bare the wooden structure of the church.

Most interesting are the exquisite paintings by Giandomenico Tiepolo, all throughout. This includes his Oratory of the Crucifix, a large number of paintings created that tell the complete story of Jesus' final days on Earth.

Tiepolo's sublime creations earned him the utmost noteriety as a Renaissance artist.

The second largest Campo behind St. Mark's Square, it is usually populated with local children playing ball. The main path runs along one side giving tourists a glimpse into daily Venetian life.

QUEST ITEM

This bottom-heavy doorway is shaped thusly because the barrel-makers needed to roll the wide barrels through the narrow doorway. It can be found at San Polo 456.

SAN POLO

Sestiere

CARLO GOLDONI'S HOUSE
1707 - 1793, Playwright

Bright and witty since early childhood, Carlo Goldoni was born in Venice to an apothecary father. Although he exhibited a love for plays as a young child, his father preferred that he put away his puppets and head toward a degree in law.

As a precocious teenager, he ran away with a band of performing strolling minstrels. On another occasion, he wrote a play that humiliated some local girls *("il Colosso")* and was once again seriously admonished.

Portrait of Goldoni, pastel on paper, around 1750, La Scala Theatre Museum, Milan

Mindful of his father's wishes, Carlo procured a degree in law, all-the-while reading plays and visiting the theatre whenever he could. While in school, he was arrested for going to a brothel. Later, he ran from an undesirable marriage to Milan, then Verona. There, he met Nicolette Conio, with whom he fell in love and ultimately married.

Back in Venice, he wrote plenty of plays, and eventually partnered with Baldassare Galuppi, a musical composer who would write the scores to Goldoni's libretto. Together, they produced more than twenty librettos.

Early on, Goldoni felt the public taste for theatre needed to evolve. The typical kind of play touted mockery, buffoonery, or flights of fancy, all of which used masks - lots of masks. Carlo's own style, although humorous to the rare point of sarcasm, was more realistic. He preferred to write about modern people and situations of the burgeoning middle-class - and he rarely used masks!

The ground floor of Casa Goldoni, with Gothic-styling and Istrian handrails.

For this he earned high praise and a special position in the community.

The public continued to hold tightly to the fastastical works of rival playwright Carlo Gozzi, so Goldoni packed up and moved to France. He continued to write and produce, and his work achieved high praise there as well. Goldini remained in France until he died blind and penniless, at the age of 85. His wife Nicolette was left to beg for a pension, so as not to starve alone in the streets.

This *stage, from the Grimani ai Servi collection, has been used as a training stage, an educational prop, and a means of in*stant entertainment.

A co*stume from Goldoni's play "Il Giocatore" (The Gambler).

SAN POLO

Sestiere

SAN ROCCO
Scuola Grande

Grand view of the Sala Superiore.

Founded in 1478, a local Confraternity chose this site next to the Church of San Rocco to build their Scuola. The building was designed in 1515 but, due to the deaths of several builders, it was not completed until 1560.

San Rocco, or Saint Roch, or Saint Rock, is the patron saint of the plague - and of dogs.

According to legend, Roch would religiously tend to diseased victims. When he himself fell ill, he retreated to the forest where a dog found him, brought him some bread, and licked his wounds until they healed.

The Scuola Grande San Rocco is a lush environment that boasts of the thousands of hours that the venerated mannerist artist Tintoretto spent as he decorated the interior of the building with his brushes. Lushly created, his works cover nearly every space the building had to offer.

Upstairs in the Sala Superiore, the meetings of the Confraternity would meet. In this room, Tintoretto created 13 ceiling paintings, and 10 wall paintings. These are highly regarded as some of his overall best works.

SAN POLO

"The Resurrection of Christ"
Tintoretto, c.1579-81, Oil on canvas

"The Last Supper"
Tintoretto, c. 1579-81, Oil on canvas

The Delights of Baccalà

Baccalà is a popular appetizer in Venice. Made from a Norwegian stock fish (cod), it is served on bread and should be enjoyed with a glass of Prosecco or a cool afternoon Aperol Spritz. This is truly a local delicacy, and one that many visitors find easy to appreciate.

Sestiere

"Crucifixion" Oil on canvas. Tintoretto c.1565. In the Sala dell'Albergo, San Rocco

SAN POLO

Sestiere

Santa Maria GLORIOSA dei FRARI

Sitting proudly in the heart of the San Polo sestiere, is the Basilica di Santa Maria Gloriosa dei Frari. After the Franciscans received an approved land grant in 1258, it took another 80-some years to complete the building of the church. Although plain on the outside, as are many Venetian churches, the inside boasts an exquisite implementation of Venetian Gothic architecture. It has the only remaining rood screens in Venice today. It also boasts the second tallest Campanile (bell tower) in the city, behind the bell tower in Saint Mark's Square.

Besides the stunning architecture, you will be treated to some of the best artworks in Venice: works by Donatello, Bellini, Titian, Sansovino, and a host of others. Additionally, an assortment of Tombs of past Doges, whose names you might see around the city: Foscari, Pesaro, and Dandolo. A beautiful monument and the tomb of the venerated Venetian painter Titian can be found in the Frari as well.

The Frari will be one of the most important Basilica's you will visit in Venice, but please allow extra time for your eyes to feast on the large selection of stunning artwork.

Saint John the Baptist by Donatello 1438. Carved wood and paint.

This "Pieta" was Titian's last painting. The poignancy of the scene after Mary and Nicodimus (with the help of a handmaiden) remove the body of Jesus from the crucifix.

Titian was interred in Santa Maria Gloriosa dei Frari where you will find his monument. Titian is depicted with the allegories of universal nature on his right, the spirit of knowledge on his left.

THE SCUOLA GRANDE

San Marco

San Rocco

Santa Maria della Misericordia

The Scuola Grandi began during the medieval times as neighborhood confraternities where their members could worship their patron Saint, and provide charitable interests to the lay population, as needed. Over the centuries, the Scuola evolved from neighborhood charitable organizations to high-bred social organizations, whose members were the social and financial elite of Venice.

They all had the appreciation for music in common, and most provided a learning environment for the musically inclined. The leading architects were hired to design the Scuola, and the best artists in the city were commissioned to decorate their interiors.

By the 1500s there were seven Scuola Grandi that were at the height of civic leadership and local government influence. Today you will find six Scuola. The seventh, Santa Maria della Carità has transformed into the Gallerie dell'Accademia, the most important museum in the City of Venice.

San Giovanni Evangelista

San Teodoro

dei Carmini

SAN GIOVANNI EVANGELISTA
Scuola Grande

This is one of the oldest Scuola Grandi in Venice. Its Confraternity was set up by flagellants to do charitable works in the city. It became famous for possessing a relic of the "True Cross" acquired as a gift from Filippo Maser, the Chancellor of the City of Jerusalem. This gift brought fame and fortune to the Confraternity, attracting both wealthy members and the money they brought with them.

The Scuola Grande is also famous for the miracle that is still told by the locals: The Relic of the True Cross had accidentally fallen into the canal but floated above the water avoiding all those that attempted to retrieve it. The exception was when Andrea Vendramin dove into the water and saved it. Andrea was the person who originally accepted the gift from the Chancellor the year prior, and he was apparently the only person that was allowed to retrieve it.

Today, a visit to San Giovanni will treat you with a myriad of excellent works, many depicting this miracle from the likes of

Titian, Tiepolo, Bellini, and Carpaccio, among many others. Note the unique and functional outdoor atrium created by the architect Pietro Lombardo.

Members of the Vendramin Family "Venerating a Relic of the True Cross," Titian and workshop, mid-1540s

LEONARDO da VINCI MUSEUM

This lovely museum is dedicated to one of the most favored people in human history: Leonardo da Vinci. A brilliant man that surpassed most experts in the many areas that interested him, he is considered to be a genius, a polymath, and a man with sensibilities and sensitivities that surpassed ordinary men.

The museum uses multimedia techniques to enhance each of da Vinci's inventions, thoughts, and discoveries, which greatly enhances a visitor's ability to understand his machines. A gem of a dedication to a giant of a man.

Leonardo da Vinci
1452 - 1519

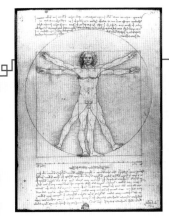

Vitruvian Man

Vitruvius was a Roman architect, author, engineer, and philosopher. He described the perfect building as possessing three principles: it must be solid (well-built), it must have utile (usability, functionality), and it must be beautiful. To da Vinci, these principles define the Divine Proportions **208**, as does the human form. This is what spurred him to create this drawing that has now become synonymous with his own name. This can be found in the Accademia **138**.

Many of da Vinci's machines were ingeniously concocted by this brilliant man, centuries before they were re-invented by someone else.
Left: an armored tank, right: automatic pulley system.

DORSODURO SESTIERE

DORSODURO

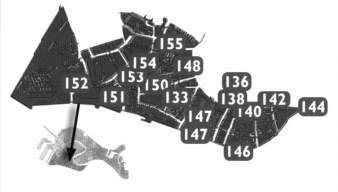

A short walk over the Accademia Bridge from Saint Mark's square will quickly find you away from the smashing crowds and among the locals. With some of the most interesting museums (the Accademia, the Guggenheim collection, and Ca'Rezzonico) and Churches (Santa Maria della Salute and San Sebastiano), Dorsoduro is a favorite getaway while in Venice. The large Campo San Margherita is loved for its local night life, and the Squero at San Trovaso, where Gondolas are hand-manufactured, will be both educational, as well as entertaining. Campo Barnaba is another local area lined with shops and restaurants for the local. Right around the corner is the Bridge of Fists (yes, they held real fist fights on this bridge), and the local fruit boat where you can enjoy a cold, fresh snack on a hot afternoon. The Scuola Grande dei Carmini is in Dorsoduro, and the University Foscari will show you how learning is accomplished today. Chiesa San Nicolo dei Mendicoli has recently uncovered ancient paintings in its attic, and a stroll along the Zattare promenade is where you will want to finish your day, grab a Spritz, and enjoy the sunset.

144 Punta della Dogana

This refers to the triangular-shaped building where the Grand Canal joins with the Giudecca Canal. Completed in 1682, it once served as the Customs House for the city of Venice. Today, it is a museum of art with a changing calendar of exhibits, including major exhibits during the Art Biennale. The Atlases on top represents the supremacy of Venice to newcomers to the city. The top figure is a wind vane, always pointing into the wind.

Sestiere

Ponte dell'Accademia 136

From atop this bridge you will enjoy some of the best views of the Grand Canal in both directions. This wooden beauty will transport you from the bustling crowds of San Marco to the quieter, more locally enjoyable side of Dorsoduro. This is a great place to take a great sunset photo over the Grand Canal!

Gallerie dell'Accademia 138

The most important museum in Venice houses pre-nineteenth century art. Inside, you will find many of the Venetian Renaissance Masters including Titian, Tiepolo, Tintoretto, and Veronese. You will also see Leonardo da Vinci's drawing of The Vitruvian Man here. This is an excellent way to spend a hot afternoon!

Peggy Guggenheim Gallery 140

For over 30 years, this facility was the home of Peggy Guggenheim. She began collecting and displaying her favorite pieces of modern art from her friends such as Pablo Picasso, Andy Warhol, and Jackson Pollack, among others. The exhibit encompasses works of abstract expressionism, cubism, and surrealism. Rt: Pablo Picasso "The Poet" 1911, oil on linen.

Santa Maria della Salute 142

A severe form of the plague overwhelmed Venice in 1630, and within one year, 30% of her people were lost, In response, the city promised to build a church to honor good health. Inside most of the artwork reflects the horrific experiences of the locals as they watched their loved ones fall to the dreaded plague.

DORSODURO

Sestiere

DORSODURO

Sestiere

146 # Fondamenta delle Zattere

A short walk over the Accademia bridge will take you away from the crowded San Marco to a breath of fresh air as you walk the waterfront promenade of Zattere. The views across the water to the island of Giudecca are excellent, especially at sunset as you enjoy a cold spritz and a cicchetti - or two!

147 # Squero di San Trovaso

An interesting site to see is the little shop that builds, repairs, and maintains the gondolas. Situated next to the Church of San Trovaso, you can, from across the water, catch the manufacture of these fine vessels. They are still hand-crafted from real woods today just as they were centuries ago - not made from plastics or fibreglass as in other places. These are the real deal!

147 # Chiesa di San Trovaso

There is no such Saint as Trovaso; the Venetians loosely blended the names of 2 brothers: Sts. Gervasio e Protasi. The most noticeable things are the two identical façades. One faces the canal, the other faces the campo. To solve a feud between two families, they each got their own entrance of equal status. Inside, you will find several Tintoretto's including his venerated "Last Supper."

148 # Ca'Rezzonico

One of the most elegant museums in the city, it exhibits furniture, items, and art works from the 1700s. The city of Venice acquired this historic building in 1935 with the intention of using it to house the overflow from the Correr Museum. Shown here is a crowd favorite: the Veiled Woman by Antonio Corradini, c.1725 . Corradini was a master of veiling his marble figures... in marble!

Veggie Boat 133

Next to the Bridge of Fists is a Venetian way of purchasing fresh produce: the Veggie Boat. Tied in the water, she sells fresh produce for the local dinnertime meal.

NOTE: On the end of this boat is an old painting of a typical fist-fight on the Bridge of Fists just beyond.

Ponte dei Pugni: Bridge of Fists 150

On top of the bridge where the man is standing, there are 4 footprints made from Istrian marble, one in each corner. Contenders would stand properly in each corner to begin the fight. The object was to knock one another into the water, but when all sense broke loose, hoards of people would mount the bridge to fight.

Chiesa di San Sebastiano 151

Listed as one of the great Plague churches in Venice, the interior is lined with fantastic paintings by Veronese who spent decades decorating the inside. Additionally, paintings by Titian and Tintoretto are found inside. In the 1500s the plague was seen as a divine punishment. This is illustrated throughout San Sebastiano.

Chiesa San Nicolò dei Mendicoli 152

LOST FRESCOES DISCOVERED
Built in the 1100s it is one of the oldest and most 'Venetian' churches in Venice. Its Byzantine-Venetian architecture has suffered many disasters, including a major flood. During a recent archaeological restoration, a lost fresco of the Crucifixion (c. 1300s) was found hiding behind a wall in the upstairs attic.

DORSODURO

Sestiere

DORSODURO

Sestiere

153 Scuola Grande Santa Maria dei Carmini

Built in 1286, it is located in Campo Santa Margherita. It was built as a church by the Carmelite monks, then closed by Napoleon and reopened by the Austrians. It demonstrates the good relationship between the Confraternity and the order. This was the last Scuola Grande to be recognized by the Council of Ten in 1597. Of special note is the trompe l'oeil tile floor.

154 Campo Santa Margherita

This is the third largest campo (behind San Marco and San Polo), and is largely appreciated for the youthful night life. Lined by local bars and restaurants with al fresco seating, Santa Margherita is one of the best places to enjoy the daily living of the local Venetians. The food is Venetian and the spritzes are quite well-priced, making this an ideal place to end the day and enjoy your evening meal.

A Fall from Grace

Legend has it that the famous artist Fumiani fell from the scaffolding in the church of San Pantalon as he finished his mega-sized painting. The locals still tell this story, although historians say otherwise.

155 Chiesa di San Pantalon

Across a bridge from Campo Santa Margherita is the little church of San Pantalon. Remarkable is the huge painting on the ceiling inside: artist Giovanni Antonio Fumiani used the architectural design of the church to create a Trompe l'oeil of magnificent proportions. It is listed as the largest canvas painting in the world. Legends (falsely) tell that Fumiani fell from the scaffolding of this church to his death.

DORSODURO

Sestiere

PONTE Dell'ACCADEMIA

DORSODURO

Sestiere

> "Over a bridge from San Sebastian is Calle Lunga San Barnaba, a narrow alleyway lined with some of Venice's most affordable pizzerias and osterie (a small local restaurant) specialising in meat dishes – a rarity in this lagoon city." from BBC

Standing on the Accademia Museum side of the bridge gives you a great view of the underside of the bridge. The steel under-structure is readily visible.

DORSODURO Sestiere

With Baldassare Longhena's monumental church of Santa Maria della Salute creating a breathtaking background, you may never want to leave this bridge! So don't. Stay until sunset and you will be rewarded with yet another scenic wonder.

The Ponte dell'Accademia, Accademia Bridge, is a quick and easy way to walk from the San Marco Sestiere to the Dorsoduro Sestiere, where it concludes at the Accademia Museum. It is one of only four bridges that span the Grand Canal.

A bridge in this area was first proposed way back in 1488, but was laughed out of the decision-making process. Centuries later, an iron bridge was installed by the Austrians, but was later demolished in 1933. A competition was held for the best design of a new bridge, but because none of the entries were approved, a wooden bridge was temporarily installed. They wanted to install a bridge that is similar to the Scalzi Bridge, but the war came along and the idea (budget) fell through the cracks.

In the late 20th century, it became necessary to reinforce the wooden bridge with a steel underbelly to give it the much-need strength while maintaining its wooden appearance. Visitors often attach "love locks" to the bridge, throwing the key into canal to seal their eternal love to their "someone special." Local authorities have attempted to crack down on this practice.

GALLERIE DELL'ACCADEMIA

DORSODURO

Founded in 1750 as an art restoration institution, the Accademia boasts the most famous and accomplished Venetian artists to be found anywhere. The first President was Giambattista Tiepolo, the Rococo master that brought the arts to new heights.

The School of Charity, the Convent of the Lateran Canons, and the church of Santa Maria della Carità (a Scuola Grande) were the three original buildings on this site, and have since been converted into the Accademia cluster that are in this spot now.

As a museum gallery today, it houses pre-nineteenth century artworks. Included are pieces by: Bastiani, Gentile and Giovanni Bellini, Bosch, Canaletto, Carpaccio, Carriera, Gaspari, Giambono, Giorgione, Longhi, Lotto, Tiepolo, Tintoretto, Titian, Veronese, Vasari, and da Vinci, to name a few.

Sestiere

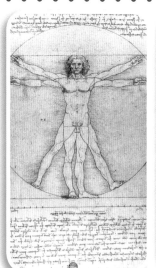

"Stealing St. Mark's Body" Tintoretto   *da Vinci's Vetruvian Man*   *"St. John the Baptist" Titian*

"Miracle of the Slave" - *Created for the Scuola Grande San Marco as part of a trilogy (including Finding the Body of San Marco, and The Abduction of San Marco's Body). Tintoretto was a mere 30 years old when he created this masterpiece.*

"The Miracle of the Slave"
Oil on Canvas, Tintoretto, c. 1548

A slave wanted to go to San Marco to see the relic of St. Mark. His master said "no," but the slave went anyway. When there, he swore an oath of loyalty to Saint Mark, and upon his return, his master wanted him to be punished. So he ordered his men to gouge out the slave's eyes, but when they tried, the stick broke. He then ordered them to cut off his legs, but the axe broke. Undaunted, the master told his men to pound his mouth so that he can no longer call to St. Mark, but too, the hammer broke.

Commissioner of the painting   *Broken stick*   *Axe being weilded*   *Broken axe*   *Broken hammer*   *St. Mark protecting the slave*   *Broken hammer*   *Master of the slave*

A growingly astonished crowd looks on as a House Master give orders to disfigure the slave. A foreshortened **217** *St. Mark in a billowing gold cape lovingly protects the slave. Tintoretto's trademark use of color and drama are evident in this painting. It appears that people of international origin are included in the audience. This could be because traders from various cultures were often seen in Venice at the time of the painting. Or perhaps Tintoretto wanted this painting not to be specifically for Venice, but for the world in general.*

DORSODURO

Sestiere

PEGGY GUGGENHEIM
1898 - 1979, Art Collector, Afficionado

Born Marguerite Guggenheim in New York City in 1898, Peggy was a member of the wealthy Guggenheim family and daughter of Benjamin Guggenheim & Florette Seligman.

Her father died in the tragic sinking of the RMS Titanic when Peggy was thirteen years old. The tragedies did not stop there. Her daughter committed suicide at forty-two years of age. Peggy survived a sister that died during childbirth, and the children of her other sister inexplicably and tragically fell off the top of a hotel building in New York City.

Peggy Guggenheim 1937

Nothing was to stop Peggy and her addiction to art collecting. Although she had no formal education in art appreciation or art history, Guggenheim managed to gather around her the people that could teach her what she needed to know.

This defined her character beautifully: Grit. She knew the right questions to ask and to whom to ask those questions. She was adamantly loyal when she backed unknown artists that she would discover during her travels. When experts told her that her taste was of an amateur at best, Peggy persisted in her choices and moved forward. She had a reputation for being a loose woman, a hanger-on in the art world, a wanna-be art aficionado, but she stuck to her guns and knew what she liked.

In 1947, she purchased a Palazzo, Vernier dei Leoni, on the Grand Canal in Venice and amassed a large collection of Lhasa Apsos that would follow her around en masse. Her little villa soon became both a well-known party house as well as the place where she would hold private gallery showings.

Her taste ran toward modernism, with a particular love of cubism. Over the years, she admired, collected, and championed the works of a great many artists that today are considered to be creators of some of the most exquisite works of the 20th century. These includ-

DORSODURO

Sestiere

GUGGENHEIM MUSEUM
Dorsoduro, 701-704, 30123 Venezia

ed Jackson Pollack, Pablo Picasso, Dali, Chagall, Marcel Duchamp, Andy Warhol, and Max Ernst, among a great many others.

Peggy lived in her home in Venice until her death at age 81. Her villa, Vernier dei Leoni, has since been converted into the Guggenheim Museum in Venice, and is where her ashes are interred in the back yard next to her fourteen beloved Lhasa Apsos.

QUEST ITEM
Saint George was a guard for the Roman Emperor Diocletian. He was martyred during the Christian Persecutions. He is best known for slaying a dragon - and rescuing the girl!

As you are enjoying your gelato-walk along the Zattere, see if you can spot, on a wall, this beautiful high relief of St. George slaying that dragon!

DORSODURO

Sestiere

SANTA MARIA della SALUTE

DORSODURO

In 1630, Venice's huge population of 146,000 was smothered with a particularly destructive form of the bubonic plague. 49,000 people died; a staggering 16,000 citizens were lost in a single month! Venice was vulnerable to such outbreaks because of their constant exposure to outsiders, many due to their success in the international trade scene.

This stunning landmark of Santa Maria della Salute is the latest of what Venice calls the **"Plague Churches."** Consecrated in 1681, it was created as a tribute to the deliverance from the Plague and carries the status of a minor Basilica.

The church was dedicated to Mary because she was not merely a patron saint of the plague, but she was considered to be a protector of the Venetian Republic itself.

A striking member of the Venetian skyline, Santa Maria della Salute, when viewed closely will show the exquisite detail of her Baroque-styling that sprung from the imagination of the 33-year-old architect Baldessarre Longhena. Sadly, Longhena died before the church was finished.

The octagonally-shaped structure was built upon 1,000,000 wooden pilings, and Istrian stone was used for its construction.

The interior floor is laid with a mesmerizing mosaic, and the high altar showcases an exceptional Baroque sculpture of the Madonna expelling the plague. It was created by the Flemish artist Josse de Corte, and replaces a sculpture that was originally commissioned to Bernini. The sculpture was brought from Crete in approximately 1600 when Herakleon was lost to the Ottomans.

La Salute is the last of the major constructions commissioned by the city of Venice and deserves a slice of your itinerary for your enjoyment.

Sestiere

Every November, the **Festa della Madonna della Salute** is held in Venice. The city builds a temporary bridge so that people can cross to La Salute with a candle to give to the Black Madonna of the Salute to ask for a miracle for a family member who may be ill. Thousands of people stand in line with a candle, awaiting their turn to cross.

When you say "Salute" while clinking your glass with a friend, you are toasting to their good health, because Salute means Health.

PUNTA della DOGANA

Punta della Dogana refers to the triangular building where the Grand Canal joins with the Giudecca Canal. Completed in 1682, it once served as the Customs House for the city of Venice. Today, it is a museum of art with a changing calendar of exhibits, including major exhibits during the Art Biennale.

The Atlases on top represent the supremacy of Venice to newcomers to the city. The top figure is a wind vane, always pointing into the wind.

FONDAMENTE ZATTERE

Zattere is an unusual site in Venice, a city where most of the streets are tiny, narrow, and surrounded by shops and buildings on all sides. Zattere is a wide fondamente that stretches along the south side of the city and offers some of the best places for a happy hour wind-down.

Several waterside eateries are scattered along the coastline, creating a great place to cool off and enjoy the spectacular view of the island of Giudecca 172 just across the lagoon ~ especially at sunset!

Zattere is where the temporary bridge is built across this same lagoon during the Festival della Redentore 279 each year. This new bridge stretches all the way across the water and terminates at the beautiful domed Redentore church on Giudecca.

If you happen to be taking a Vaporetto ride around the island, there is a Zattere stop where you might feel obligated to stroll the wide waterfront street and enjoy an Aperol Spritz.

SQUERO di SAN TROVASO

Next to the two-faced Church of San Trovaso is the Squero di San Trovaso. This is an authentic gondola shop, where gondolas are constructed and maintained. A walk around the back side may offer you a glimpse inside where Venetian craftsmen are custom-crafting new boats for their new customers. Although gondolas may be seen in other parts of the world, authentic gondolas are made only in Venice.

CHIESA di SAN TROVASO
The Two-Faced Church

Initially built in the 11th century, rebuilt in the 16th century, and consecrated in the 17th century, this unconventional little church tells some interesting stories. To begin with, there is no such Saint as *"Trovaso."* The Venetians loosely blended the names of two brother saints Gervasio e Protasi. Some say that the unusual two identical façades of this church

represent these two brothers. However, these two façades, one which faces the canal and the other which faces the campo, were actually created to solve a feud between two families. Although both families attended San Travaso, they each got their own entrance of equal status, and therefore, could enter and exit without having the unpleasant fortune of encountering each other or their families in passing. Inside you will find several Tintoretto's including his venerated *"Last Supper"* in the Santissimo Chapel. *"Temptations of Saint Anthony Abbot"* by Jacopo Tintoretto is mounted in the rear chapel.

DORSODURO

Sestiere

DORSODURO

CA' REZZONICO

Ca'Rezzonico, on the banks of the Grand Canal in Dorsoduro Sestiere, is a delightful display of Baroque and Roccoco art from the 18th century. Since the Baroque styling of Baldesarre Longhena was replacing the taste for Renaissance or Palladian architecture in Venice, Longhena was brought in to design Ca'Rezzonico.

Sestiere

The most impressive room in the building is the Grand Ballroom. Superbly decorated in Baroque gilting, the ceiling centerpiece is a fresco "Chariot of Apollo" by Giovanni Battista Crosato, above. Pieces to note throughout are Tiepolo's "Nobility and Virtue defeating Ignorance," "Allegory of Merit" by Mattia Bortoloni, and Canaletto's "Views of the Grand Canal." A crowd favorite is the delicate sculpture of the "Veiled Woman" *(below)* by Antonio Corradini. It is common to stare at her and wonder how he was able to create a transparent veil from stone. Truly remarkable!

A Blaze of Colored Lights

In the 1920's, Cole Porter leased Ca'Rezzonico for approximately $4,000 per month. He hosted a party where his hired tight-rope walkers plus 50 gondoliers all performed in "a blaze of colored Lights."

~*Billboard Magazine, 1949*

DORSODURO

Sestiere

149

PONTE dei PUGNI *(Bridge of Fists)*

DORSODURO

Once upon a time, there were two rival families, the Nocolotti and the Castellani. Every year between September and December, they would face-off with one another in the "War of the Punches." Locals would fill the canal, the streets, and the rooftops as they rooted for their faction. Back then, there were no balustrades *(railings)* on the bridge, and contenders often fell to the dirty waters below. Today when you walk across this bridge, note the footprints in the corners. This is where the contenders would stand to begin the fights. These fights continued for generations, but were ultimately outlawed in 1705 due to the fact that it got so rough that people were being killed.

"Competition on the Ponte dei Pugni" Joseph Heitz, c. 1673

Sestiere

CHIESA di SAN SEBASTIANO

Listed as one of the great Plague churches in Venice, this Renaissance beauty was first built in 1393 as a hospice, then rebuilt in 1468 as a church and dedicated to Saint Sebastian.

The plague was viewed as a divine punishment, and this church, along with 4 others, was built to calm the divinity and as a plea for the end of the plague.

The legend of Saint Sebastian tells that he was martyred in 288ce during the persecution of Christians by Diocletian. Many artworks depict him tied to a tree or a post as he is barraged with arrows. Others tell that he was saved by Irene of Rome, then later clubbed to death by Diocletian's men.

Chiesa di San Sebastiano is a tiny parish church that is covered from floor to ceiling with masterpieces painted over three decades by Paolo Veronese. Legend has it that the Renaissance master found refuge here after fleeing murder charges in his hometown of Verona in 1555 and lavished this church with his gratitude.

"The Martyrdom of Saint Sebastian"
Paolo Veronese 1558, fresco

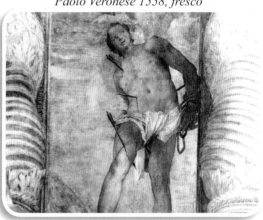

"The Coronation of the Virgin"
Paolo Veronese (1528–1588)

DORSODURO

Sestiere

151

SAN NICOLO dei MENDICOLI

Tucked quietly away in the working-class neighborhood of Dor-soduro is probably the most quaint church in Venice. Unlike the grand Palazzo-like churches and basilicas that dot Venice, this is your grandmother's church. It's warmth and charm make it quite approachable and easy to relax in.

Saint Nicolas was the Patron Saint of boats, mariners, and the sea. This is probably why the local fishermen loved him so much. Yes, this is the same Saint Nicolas that became the Santa Claus that we all know today.

A local legend tells that a poor priest built this church to cover an even older church that used to stand in this place. When the local authorities asked him where he acquired the money to build the church, he replied that there used to be an ancient monument to Venus here, and where the tower is now, he had found the money buried in the earth.

An Archaeological Surprise

When the church was recently being restored after seri-ous flood damage, the construction crew were reinforcing the attic when they uncovered this ancient pre-Renaissance fresco (circa 1300s), of the Crucifixion *(above-right)*. The artist is currently unknown. This was a fantastic surprise for the church! This room cannot be opened to the public until archaeological restorations have been completed, and the existing paintings are protected.

SANTA MARIA dei CARMINI
Scuola Grande

Built in 1286 by Francesco Caustello and Baldassare Long-hena, it is located in Campo Santa Margherita. It was built as a church by the Carmelite monks, then closed by Napoleon decree, then reopened again by the Austrians. It demonstrates the good relationship between the Confraternity and the order. This was the last of the seven Scuola Grande to be recognized by the Council of Ten in 1597. Of special note is the trompe l'oeil mosaic tile floor.

This stunning Baroque-styled corridor is a detailed work of elegance as it floats above, seemingly cloud-like. Below is a trompe l'oeil tiled floor that gives a completely different feel than the florets that float above.

DORSODURO

Sestiere

153

CAMPO SANTA MARGHERITA

DORSODURO

Sestiere

Dorsoduro is the artsy, bohemian Sestiere of Venice. Campo Santa Margherita is an eclectic mixture of the real Venetian locals, the modern flavors of the nearby University students, and of course, the drizzling of global tourists.

It is the locals that give the real flavor to Santa Margherita. In the afternoons, you may find locals hanging out sipping a wine and sharing old stories. Across the way, you might see a band of students studying for an upcoming test. On Sunday mornings, you will see the locals as they pour forth from the churches and began their after-church socializing. Of course, there are the flower vendors accompanied by booths selling everything thing from fresh fruits to socks.

In any case, unless there is a highly visible event going on, Santa Margherita is a place where you won't see a huge influx of tourists.

SAN PANTALON

DORSODURO

Sestiere

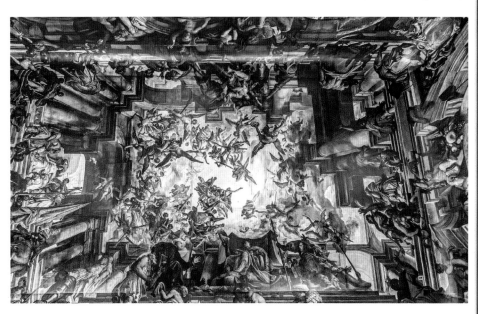

Across a bridge from Campo Santa Margherita is the little church of San Pantalon. Remarkable is the huge painting on the ceiling inside: artist Giovanni Antonio Fumiani used the architectural design of the church to create a Trompe l'oeil of magnificent proportions. It is listed as the largest canvas painting in the world.

Legends (falsely) tell that Fumiani fell from the scaffolding of this church to his death. Other research shows that he was alive well, after this incident was supposed to have taken place. Nevertheless, this ceiling will astound you with its expert use of vanishing point perspective, a technique that was revitalized after a one thousand-year disappearance, by Filippo Brunelleschi in Florence in the early 1400s. Brunelleschi used it for creating the plans and drawings that were needed to accurately construct the Duomo over Santa Maria del Fiore in Florence, which helped to define the early days of the Renaissance.

QUEST

Do you dare to find this Campiello? The incurables were those who were diagnosed with an incurable disease - such as the plague - and who were waiting to die. Situated quietly within the confines of Dorsoduro, I hope this does not become your future home!

SANTA CROCE SESTIERE

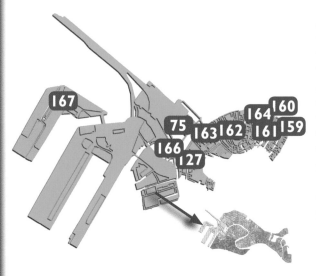

All transportation enters and leaves Venice from Santa Croce. This includes trains, buses, and automobiles. Santa Croce is unique from the other Sestieri in its variety of neighborhoods within. You will find some of the best museums of Venice along the Grand Canal portion of Santa Croce. Find quiet, local areas of apartments, shops, and the most pleasant eateries.

As you approach the transportation hub that includes the Santa Maria train station and Piazzale Roma, you'll find that the shops and restaurants suddenly become more touristy, and ergo, pricier. You'll notice that the crowds are more harried as they attempt to pull their suitcases over the cobbles and bridges. A rare sight in Venice are green parks. Papadopoli Gardens is a wonderful respite for tired feet, shade, or a picnic.

If you are traveling with kids, check out the Museum of Natural History. Not your typical museum, they will most certainly enjoy the Room of Curiosities. Santa Croce is alive with music and outdoor events, and boasts plenty of dining al fresco to assist in your people-watching hobby. You'll find plenty of family-life here, with a wide variety of activities plus wonderful local churches to keep everyone busy and happy.

The Butcher of Santa Croce

Along the Grand Canal there used to be a small butchery that was famous for their meats and sausages. The owner, Biasio, had a secret recipe that the neighborhood loved. One day, a customer found something odd on his plate. Upon a closer look, he saw that it was the finger of a child! Biasio was a serial killer that was putting them in his sausages! The horrified city cheered when Biasio was dragged by horse to the prisons, his hands were cut off, and he was executed in Saint Mark's Square for everyone to see. Today in the place of his restaurant is the Riva de Biasio Vaporetto stop that marks this horrifying episode in Venice's already colorful history.

Ca'Pesaro

Completed in 1710, the building boasts a huge double-columned Baroque format facing the Grand Canal. The inside displays modern art from the 19th and 20th centuries: from major Venetian, Italian and international painters to well-known Italian statuary. Upstairs, you will find an important Oriental Art Museum.

San Stae 160

Its brief name is a shortening from Saint Eustachius. Built during the 11th century, it was rebuilt in the 1600s in this elegantly intricate Baroque style. Inside you will find the tomb for the Mocenigo family, along with excellent paintings by Tiepello, Bambini, del Vecchia, and many others. Placed carefully about is a great variety of statuary from sculptors, such as Antonio Corradini.

Natural History Museum 161

The study of the historical flora and fauna of the Venice Lagoon is on display. Undersea specimens, birds. and animals small and large. A strange collection of taxidermy will spur your imagination. This is a perfect and inexpensive way to retreat from the crowds out on the streets.

San Giacomo dell'Orio 162

The history of this church is not completely known, but it appears that it was built in 800s, then rebuilt several times since. Inside, several esteemed works of art by Bassano, Veneziano, and the altarpiece by Veronese all live under the ship's keel ceiling, which of itself is its own marvel.

SANTA CROCE

Sestiere

Sestiere

163 Tombs of Chiesa di San Simeone Piccolo

Also known as San Simeone e Giuda, this little dome will be seen on your right as you begin your Grand Canal ride after boarding the Vaporetto at Piazzale Roma. The tombs await your visit!

164 Mocenigo Palace

A delightful exhibit of the sophisticated fashion of Venice's past. An exhibit was added that boasts of the world of fine fragrances. Trace the route from the flower, plant, or seed origins to the final perfumes that Venice has been known for globally.

158 Papadopoli Gardens

The Santa Croce Monastery that once stood here, was closed during the Napoleonic era. Today, it provides a public respite for tired souls/soles. Parks are rare here, and Papadopoli is easy to access.

166 Piazzale Roma

Piazzale Roma is where the mainland buses connect to the island Vaporetti. Passengers board the Vaporetto boat for transport to the appropriate neighborhoods on the islands of Venice, Murano, Burano, and Lido.

110 Ponte della Costituzione

This bridge connects the main transportation hubs on the Tronchetto. It joins the Santa Lucia train station on Cannaregio to the bus station and the main boat dock on Santa Croce. It is the newest bridge in Venice.

167 Tronchetto

*The Tronchetto connects the large ships to the island of Venice. Once here you can ride the **People Mover** (overhead rail) to Piazzale Roma, where you can either take a bus to the mainland, or board a Vaporetto.*

CA' PESARO

Built in the late 1600s for the Pesaro family, its Baroque-style was designed by Baldassarre Longhena, the Venetian architect known for his work on Santa Maria della Salute and Ca'Rezzonico, among many others.

The grand palace, now the seat of the Galleria Nazionale d'Arte Moderna, was built in the second half of the seventeenth century for the noble and wealthy Pesaro family. Work began in 1659 starting from the landside; the courtyard, with its striking loggias, was completed by 1676; the splendid façade on the Grand Canal had already reached the second floor by 1679, but, on Longhena's death in 1682, the palace was still unfinished. The Pesaro family entrusted its completion to Gian Antonio Gaspari who concluded it in 1710, in compliance with the original project.

The collection of works from nineteenth-century Venice is quite remarkable and has been enriched over the years by further acquisitions and donations. In 1914, a number of notable works in wax by Medardo Rosso were acquired increasing the overall depth of the collection in this grandiose palace.

"The Thinker" by Auguste Rodin, 880,
Polished plaster; Permanent exhibit.
Gift / Donated by Filippo Grimani, 1907

SANTA CROCE

Sestiere

SAN STAE

Its brief name is a shortening from Saint Eustachius. Built during the 11th
century, this church was
rebuilt in the 1600s in the
elegantly intricate Ba-
roque-style. Inside, you
will find the tomb for the
Mocenigo family, along
with excellent paintings
by Tiepello, Bambini, del
Vecchio, and many others.
Placed carefully about is
a great variety of statu-
ary from sculptors such as
Antonio Corradini.

The images below are but
a small sample of the su-
perb works waiting for you
in San Stae.

"Torture of St. Thomas"
Giambattista Pittoni,
1722, Oil on canvas

"Charity"
Antonio Tarsia,
1700-1, Marble

"Martyrdom of
St. Bartholomew"
Giovanni Battista Tiepolo
1722, Oil on canvas

MUSEO di NATURAL HISTORY

The Natural History Museum of Venice:

- Promotes scientific research
- Organizes educational activities for schools
- Opens to the public a rich, naturalistic library
- Guarantees conservation, restoration, cataloging, and increasing of its naturalistic collections
- Offers educational services in the scientific-naturalistic field, through permanent and temporary exhibitions, courses and conferences, laboratories and editorial activities.

Not your typical Museum of Natural History, this museum displays several themes of nature's wonders. Included is the collection of fossilized sea creatures such as excellent trilobite specimens; a gathering of undersea life in the Cetacean gallery; the search for dinosaurs; how form and function define the strategies of life; African big game collections; and an assortment of oddities in the Room of Wonders.

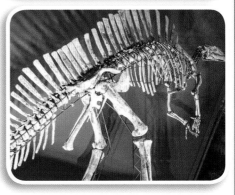

SAN GIACOMO DELL'ORIO

The history of this church is not completely known, but it appears that it was built in the 800s, then rebuilt several times since. Inside several esteemed works of art by Bassano, Veneziano, and the altar-piece by Veronese, all re-side under the ship's keel ceiling, which of itself, is its own marvel.

The Cursed Palazzo

Buried deeply within Santa Croce is the Palazzo Dario. Ca'Dario is believed to be cursed, because no less than 18 different people have suffered horrible fates after owning the building, and some from merely staying in the building. These fates included several suicides, murder, a broken leg, financial ruin, and an untimely automobile accident. It now stands unoccupied, awaiting a remodel. To disguise itself from the wretched curse, pray tell? Perhaps you will be the next owner of this accursed house!

CHIESA di SAN SIMEONE

Also known as San Simeone e Giuda, this dome will be seen on your right as you begin your Grand Canal ride, after boarding the Vaporetto at Piazzale Roma and before crossing under the Scalzi Bridge. The little church, completed in 1738, is one of the youngest in Venice and has been called one of the ugliest churches in Venice. Beneath its foundation hides a little-known secret: **a 21-tomb crypt.** Four hallways intersect into an octagonal room, all walls covered in frescoes. If asked, the Keeper will give you a candle to take on your little journey down into the mysterious depths to visit the Crypts of San Simeone. If luck is on your side, you will emerge safely. Perhaps.

> *"I have seen churches without domes, but never before have I seen a dome without a church."* Napoleon Bonaparte

SANTA CROCE

Sestiere

MOCENIGO PALACE

Dedicated to the lifestyle of the 1600s-1700s Venetian Nobleman, Palazzo Mocenigo expertly recreates many aspects of his daily life and activities. Covering twenty rooms on the ground floor, you will begin to imagine what it was like to live his life here in the watery environs of Venice.

Originally designed with Gothic architecture, this structure was later altered into the building you see today. It originally housed the San Stae branch of the Mocenigo family, who were important members of the Venetian elite. In fact, seven of their family members became Doges between the years 1414 and 1778.

On display are exquisite examples of rich textiles used to make clothing, furniture, and drapery; many items of clothing that were gentlemanly-chic; furniture and a variety of well-set rooms; and six rooms dedicated to the history of perfume and the collection of rare perfume bottles are on display as well.

This is a rare and exotic display of the good life, and should not be missed while you are in Venice.

This map, on display in the museum, explains the trade routes for some of the main ingredients in perfumes. For example: saffron came from Syria, jasmine came from Egypt, nutmeg was brought from Romania, orange flower came from Morocco, and lavender came from the coast between Barcelona and Marseilles. Perfume was so important that these trade routes were well-controlled by the Venetians.

The image below shows many of the raw ingredients used in perfumery.

Workshops are held where visitors can learn about perfumery and even create a perfume of their own!

SANTA CROCE

The museum is a stunning recreation of Noble life in the 17th and 18th century. Included is the grand foyer, with frescoes and Murano 178 glass chandeliers throughout. An area of focus are the garments that were in style during that period. A Noble would have his clothing individually designed and hand-stitched by locals.

Sestiere

PIAZZALE ROMA

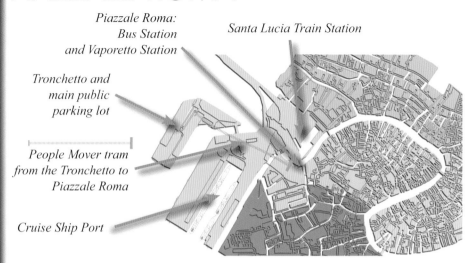

Piazzale Roma:
Bus Station
and Vaporetto Station

Santa Lucia Train Station

Tronchetto and
main public
parking lot

People Mover tram
from the Tronchetto to
Piazzale Roma

Cruise Ship Port

Piazzale Roma is the bustling center in the Santa Croce Sestiere where all modes of transportation meet on the historical island of Venice. If you arrive by air, a bus or cab will bring you to Piazzale Roma. If you travel by train, you will land on Venice, then walk over a bridge to Piazzale Roma. If you arrive by car, you will park it on the Tronchetto, then take the People Mover to Piazzale Roma for your next leg. Cruise ship visitors can easily walk over to Piazzale Roma.

What is here that you must pass through? The Vaporetto, of course. The Vaporetto, or water bus, is the main form of transportation that will bring you from the beginning of the island to all of the neighborhoods throughout the city. From here you will get your first photos of the famous leisure lifestyle of the Venetian Grand Canal.

TRONCHETTO

The iconic scenes of gondolas on the famous Venice canals are found almost immediately upon entering the neighborhood of Piazzale Roma.

The Tronchetto is the man-made island that was created to house the main parking structure for automobiles. Residents will leave their car here regularly, and visitors can purchase a parking pass for the garage. Several Port administrative buildings reside here as well.

PEOPLE MOVER

The People Mover opened in 2010 to transport people from the parking structure in the Tronchetto to the Bus Station and the Vaporetto Station at Piazzale Roma. It makes one single stop near the middle of the line to accommodate the Cruise Ship passengers.

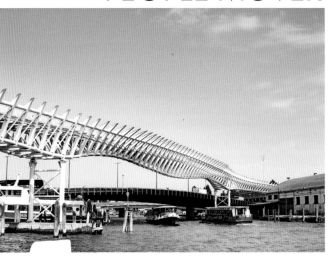

OUTER ISLANDS

When you leave the historic island city of Venice, surprises await you.

Most of the islands in the Venezia Lagoon are modern: modern houses, streets, cars, stop lights, etc. There are only a small handful of islands that have retained their ancient wonders.

The islands marked in yellow are islands that are all openly available to you; they all retain their historic environment - with the exception of Lido Island. If you aren't expecting this, getting off the boat in Lido could be a bit of a shock. As soon as you step foot on the island, a bus or taxi may go whizzing by and startle you.

172 Giudecca is a long casual stroll, a perfect thing to do as you enjoy a gelato. Walk around the back to see a few more islands in the Lagoon.

174 San Giorgio is a 5-minute Vaporetto ride from San Marco, and the visit will take you less than an hour, and when you go up into the tower... WOW!!!

176 Lido is the only non-historic island in the Venice group. Therefore, it has cars, stop lights, etc. Its main attraction is its nearly 7-mile-long white sandy beach. In addition to hosting the annual Venice Film Festival, Lido is the ideal place for sun-seeking visitors.

178 Murano - Ah, the glass! You won't be able to leave without getting at least one trinket or gift made from the most luscious glass in the world.

186 Burano is the colorful little town that dreams are made of. And the lace is a delicate art that is being lost to time.

190 Torcello is the perfect place to go for lunch. You won't regret it! While you're there, go up the tower to get a brand-new high view of the southern Lagoon!

192 San Francesco has only one place to visit: a monastery. A little bird told Saint Francis of Assisi to stop here, and so he did. A beautiful monastery was built here in his honor.

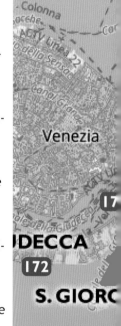

TORCELLO
190

BURANO
186

S. FRANCESCO
192

178
MURANO

THE ISLANDS
OF THE VENETIAN LAGOON

Sant'Erasmo

Le Vignole

Punta Sab

ACTV Linea 14   Lido - Punta Sabbioni

ACTV Linea 15

Aeroporto
Nicelli -
Lido

176

LIDO

OUTER ISLANDS

Venice is not simply one lone island. It is made up of 118 islands! Each island has its own distinct and unique personality. Most tourists aren't aware of their importance, so they tend to stay on the main island only. If you are looking to ditch the crowds, this is where you will want to go. These 7 islands are easy to reach by Vaporetto (water bus), are uncrowded, and are worth your while. Build in an extra day or two to visit these gems of Venice and come home with experiences that few others have taken the time to enjoy.

172 Giudecca

When standing at St. Mark's Square, look across the water to the right. That is Giudecca. An afternoon stroll will take you through local restaurants, gondola factories, and plenty of views of Venice across the Giudecca Canal. Walking to the back side will reward you with vistas of other islands, hiding behind it in the Venice Lagoon.

174 San Giorgio

From St. Mark's Square, you'll see this tower straight across the waterway. That is the island of San Giorgio. A Vaporetto will get you there quickly. See the Church of San Giorgio, the maze gardens, then go up the tower. No stairs to climb - an elevator will whisk you directly up to one of the greatest views in all of Venice.

176 Lido

California beaches in Venice? Not really. If you are in the mood to lounge by the sea, Lido is your island. With long white, sandy beaches and plenty of umbrellas, you'll return home with a great tan. If you've been on Venice for awhile, take note that Lido is the only island with cars. This could be startling if you are not expecting to see them!

Murano 178

This island is world famous for its artisanal glass products. Long ago, glass makers relocated from Turkey and Serbia to the island of Venice. They kept catching the city on fire, so they were relocated again to the island of Murano. From fine jewelry to chandeliers, you will see that today's glass-makers have clearly perfected their trade.

Burano 186

This colorful little island village is a feast for your eyes! Homes were painted with bright colors so that the fishermen could see their own home through the fog. Lace-making has grown into a competitive tradition, and because of this, you will find some of the best lace products in the world.

Torcello 190

This island is the biggest surprise of all. With a population of less than 10 citizens, this tiny island offers much to enjoy. From the scenic river walk to the climb up the tall church tower, you will find plenty to savor at a more relaxed pace than the other islands. A line-up of open scenic restaurants await you with a wonderful meal and a cold gelato finish.

San Francesco 192

This little island is all about one thing: the quaint but history-filled Monastery. In Burano, you should find a guide to take you here on a private boat. Once here, a Monk may be available to take you through the Monastery and its storied past.

OUTER ISLANDS

GIUDECCA

In antiquity, Giudecca was once an island of farming plots (as seen in Barbari's famous woodcut map made in 1500, **38**). After that, it was transformed into a mecca of factories that specialized in textiles and flour.

Giudecca is the long island that you see when you look across the lagoon from Saint Mark's Square. It runs opposite the entire length of the Sestiere of Dorsoduro. Picturesque in the sunset, it boasts a beautiful church in the middle of your view, the Church of the Redentore *(inset, far-right-top)*.

Other than the Church and the Hilton Stucky Hotel, what else is there to do/ see on Giudecca?

Giudecca is one of the last bastions of truly local Venetians. This island boasts

Il Redentore sits in the middle of Giudecca, and was built in thanks for the ending of the Black Plague. Each year, a bridge stretching from Venice to il Redentore, is erected over the lagoon, so that the Doge can walk to the church to give thanks and pray that the plague will never return to his beloved Venice.

unmatched views of the outer lagoon and a few Gondola shops that still create those exquisite black Gondolas. You won't find foreign-owned knick-knack shops here. Only a smattering of local shops, restaurants, and bars. The little stretch of water between Giudecca and Venice makes it just out of reach for the lion share of tourists.

For art lovers, Giudecca seems to be transforming itself into an art colony. Doing so quite successfully, I might add. Its quiet, virtually tourist-free environment makes it the perfect home for artists of all genres to come, think, imagine, and create. For art lovers, Giudecca is a local haven to escape the crowds and to enjoy a wide variety of galleries. Painters, sculptors, jewelers, photographers, and musicians - all seem to enjoy the secluded atmosphere of Giudecca. In fact, it has become a must-do stop for art buyers from all around the globe. Giudecca is a secret art gem where you may discover the next upcoming art superstar!

These oar-powered boats await their next racing event on the back side of Giudecca where Gondola shops still craft the Gondolas of today.

The quiet canals of Giudecca possess that Venice 'look' but lack the Venice tourist crowds.

173

VENICE

PATTY CIVALLERI

SAN GIORGIO MAGGIORE

San Giorgio Maggiore as seen from Saint Mark's Campanile (bell tower).

Saint Mark's Square

One of two boat marinas on San Giorgio Maggiore

San Giorgio Maggiore was first occupied by the Romans in antiquity. By 829, Venice had consecrated a church to St. George. In 982, Giovanni Morosini, a Benedictine Monk, petitioned the Doge to donate the island to a Monastery. He drained the island of standing water and built the Monastery of San Giorgio.

The church you see today was designed by Andrea Palladio, who as always, designed an intricately crafted Renaissance Basilica of lustrous white marble. Inside, you will find the exceptional painting of "The Last Supper" by the venerated Venetian artist, Tintoretto.

OUTER ISLANDS

Jorges Luis Borges  was a writer of philosophically-based short stories. From Argentina, he traveled the globe spending much time in Europe. His works are cherished around the world in many languages. Having gone blind at age 55, he never learned to read Braille. This maze was created in 2012 on the 25th anniversary of his death. This 1-kilometer-long maze is lined with handrails, and Braille-written signs, so that blind people today can enjoy this tribute garden to Jorges Luis Borges.

OUTER ISLANDS

LIDO

Lido is the only island within the Venetian cluster that is not included under the 'Historic City' banner. Therefore, it has cars, buses, and traffic lights like most other modern cities. Unlike most other modern cities, it has an incredible white sandy beach that stretches over five miles in length!

Lido is the 7-mile-long sand bar that forms the barrier separating and protecting Venice from the Adriatic Sea. Housing approximately 20,000 residents, the name 'Lido' is synonymous throughout Europe with 'Beach.'

The mere fact that the island is not attached to the mainland gives

it an air of exclusivity that wouldn't be achieved otherwise. Not only do tourists arrive here from around the globe, but Italian mainlanders find Lido to be a wonderful holiday stop as well.

The northern section of Lido is dominated by large and luxurious hotel properties. It is the home base for the annual Venice Film Festival, and a few random celebs enjoy calling Lido their home.

The l-o-n-g beach is lined with cabanas and sun shelters which can be rented by the day; the further north you go, the less expensive their charges become.

When you step off from the Vaporetto stop, you will immediately notice the stop lights, buses, and cars. Bearing all of the conveniences of modern-day living, it is a common beach destination for tourists all over Europe, as well as local Venetians.

OUTER ISLANDS

MURANO

Murano is a cluster of seven linked islands in the Venice Lagoon. It maintains a locally cherished reputation of housing the best-glass making artisans in the world.

Originally claimed by the Romans, Murano gained a solid foothold as a fishing village, then as a major producer of salt. The village thrived for centuries until around 1000ce when people began moving to Dorsoduro, weakening its population and independent political strength. In the 1100s monks and nuns from the Camaldolese order, in their constant quest for a solitary monastic life, settled into the once bustling - now quiet island of Murano.

The monks eventually built the Monastery of San Michele de Murano (St. Michael). Over the centuries, it became a center of higher learning. A resident, Fra Mauro, became famous as a Cartographer. He created the most detailed map of the world that had ever been seen up until that time.

Meanwhile back in 1204 on the island of Venice, Turkish glass makers that had recently fled the sack of Constantinople, were setting up shops and factories. Since Venetian traders had gained prosperity by trading the beautiful artisanal glass from the Turkish Glass Masters, these same glass artisans felt it would behoove them to move to Venice where the local traders could easily stock up and move their products out to the world. This created a wonderfully symbiotic relationship between the two parties.

Until...

Furnaces are integral to glass-making, and fires were a constant hazard to a city built of wood. The citizens of Venice became fed up with the constant accidental burning of their homes and businesses. So in 1291, the City of Venice officially moved all glass factories to the island of Murano.

Living in such close proximity to each other on such a small island created a pecking order of glass makers amongst themselves. They held regular contests for creativity, quality, and innovation. They traded ideas as well as kept them secret. Over all, this created an acceleration of innovation in glass production and quality, catapulting them far ahead of any other known glass markets in the world.

Today, tourists can visit the glass art created by families which have been creating glass masterpieces, some for nearly 800 years.

Museum of Glass

Founded in 1861, the Glass Museum houses the most complete collection of Murano glass dating back to antiquity. This building used to be the home for the Bishops of Torcello. Notice the change in the quality of the glass over the centuries as new techniques were developed.

Basilica de Santa Maria e San Donato

Built in the 600s, this is the "Duomo" of Murano. The Byzantine mosaics are stunning! In addition to the relics of Saint Donato, you will find 4 large rib bones each (approx 3 feet long) from the Dragon that Saint Donato slew during his visit to Greece.

Campo San Stefano 183

Next to the Bell Tower of San Stefano stands this exquisite "Glass Comet," a sculpture created by Simone Cenedese. "In my works there are the moments of life, those in which we find a fragment that contains an entire story." Quote from Simone Cenedese

Funkiness

Walking through the island - not just on the main roads - will reward you with the inner personality of Murano. You will come across some fun and quirky sites that will put a smile on your face. You will come away feeling like you got to know her well.

OUTER ISLANDS

OUTER ISLANDS

GLASS MUSEUM

Away from the bustling city of Venice on one of her beautiful daughter islands is the Murano Glass Museum. A member of the Civic Museum Foundation, the Glass Museum will walk you through the history of glass, as well as the trials and tribulations of the growth of the glass industry in Venice.

It was founded in 1861, during the darkest period of the glass-making industry. Back in its early days, it was partially set up as a school where glass makers would come during their off-times to learn new techniques, to practice their art, or to teach.

The museum collection grew rapidly as many locals stepped up to donate pieces of their old but beautiful glass pieces to the museum. Wealthy collectors, such as Correr, Cicogna and Molin, donated a vast majority of their family collections. Some of the most treasured pieces from the Renaissance period were donated and are still cherished today.

The museum is located in the Palazzo Giustinian near the center of Murano. Here you will enjoy a chronological visit through time as you learn how the art and the industry has grown throughout the centuries. Today, Murano glass is highly valued around the world.

OUTER ISLANDS

Glass Museum

Murano 2018
4,324 Population
1,350 Glass Workers
1500 outside Murano
50 Glass Master/Designers
50 Glass Masters
30 New Style Designers
1465 Retailers who sell Murano glass in Venice proper.

Punishable by Death
1291 ~ All Glass factories were moved to Murano. 1294 ~ A law was passed that no Glass Master was allowed to leave Murano for fear that he might teach the world the artisanal glass making secrets of Murano. The Glass Master was treated as an Elite class member, and could marry into Elite families and attend Elite functions, so long as he did not leave the island for the remainder of his life. Breaking this law was punishable by death.

Fire Makers
As the population of glass makers grew in Venice, fires around the city became too frequent for the locals to bear, as most structures in Venice are made from wood. So in 1291, the city allocated the island of Murano to be the official city of glass makers who were all moved out for the safety of the rest of the city.

OUTER ISLANDS

The History of Glass

The earliest glass to be used by man was made by nature. Created as a Volcanic by-product, obsidian has been used long before recorded history. Early people around the world used obsidian for making tools, spears & arrows, beads, and money.

According to archaeological data, the first man-made glass came from the Egyptian-Mesopotamian area around 3500bce. As a craft, it grew quickly, then waned considerably for nearly 2,000 years.

This pectoral (chest piece) found in King Tut's tomb in Egypt, was among the cache of treasures discovered by archaeologist Howard Carter in 1922. The yellow/green scarab highlighted in the center of this piece is thought to be made of desert glass (formed when a meteorite collided with Earth) that was found in the desert area of East Libya/West Egypt. 1332-1323bce.

Between 700-500bce, the interest in glass was renewed, and although the pieces were small and crude (because the furnaces were small, and raising heat temperatures high enough proved challenging), an industry was born.

Sometime during the first century, a fellow in Syria created the glass blower, thus changing the techniques and the possibilities for ever.

Later as the Venetian Republic became the trading power of the Western World, traders became wealthy in the trading of glass, forming excellent relationships with the Turkish glass artisans. Then in the early 1200s when Constantinople was being overthrown during the 4th Crusade, the glass makers felt it prudent to relocate to be nearer to their Venetian trading partners, so they fled Turkey and took up shop in Venice. This proved not to be such a great plan because they used extremely hot fires under relatively low levels of control, and of course, Venice is made of wood. A bad combination! Loss of homes and businesses became so frequent that the glass-making industry was moved to the island of Murano, where you will find them today.

• •

From the whimsical to the lavish, Murano glass makers have been creating stunning pieces that have adorned fine homes, businesses, and cities for nearly 800 years. 1. Murano glass made over the doorway for the Howey Mansion in Florida, Usa 2. People, animals, and other objects from nature are a common theme; 3. A glass maker creates a prancing horse with molten glass; 4. A beautiful sculpture adorns the Island of Burano; 5. Exquisite and delicate chandeliers are popular items that are crafted in Murano and shipped globally.

OUTER ISLANDS

BURANO

OUTER ISLANDS

A pleasant 6-mile boat ride to Burano will land you on the sweetest island in the Venetian Lagoon: Burano. Immediately you will notice the famously colorful houses along the canals, and lace shops that populate nearly every block of this 52-acre island. Why does it look this way? And why is lace so important here?

Oops, Wrong House!!!

Local islanders have always fed their families on the abundant fish in the lagoon. However, the Autumn evenings in Burano are known for getting fogged in. When the fishermen returned home at dusk (perhaps a bit inebriated), they found it difficult to find their own house which back then, were all painted white. This resulted in arguments because sometimes a fisherman would return home to the wrong house (and perhaps, as the locals tell it, to the wrong bed). Painting each house a unique bright color solved this problem.

Burano is made from four islands connected by bridges. Like Venice, canals run between the islands reminding you that Burano is part of the Venetian family of islands. The population of 2,800 residents live in brightly-hued houses that fill the islands completely, less a couple of green park areas.

It seems that the island was originally populated by the Romans in the 500s, and was administered from the island of Torcello.

In the early days, all of the homes were painted using a white lime to sanitize them. Once it was decided to use colors, they would add mineral oxides to the lime which produced a rainbow of hues. For centuries, a homeowner had to apply for a color change of their own house. The local government would decide which color they would be allowed to paint it. Today, this rule no longer applies, and an owner can choose any color they like for their home.

Each day, the men would go off to fish, leaving the women to repair their damaged nets. The ladies turned this into a social event, chatting happily while they sewed. This became competitive as the techniques became fancier and the knotting became more detailed. Eventually, the thread and the needle were so small that their creations migrated from fishing nets to tablecloths and clothing, hence the beginning of the beloved lace industry in Burano.

Museo del Merletto - Lace 188 Museum

Here you will be introduced to one of the most unique crafts in the Lagoon. A short video will show you how this began in Burano, and how it progressed into what you see today. If you are so inclined, you can try your hand at lace making. Observe the women as they craft a detailed piece of elegance right before your very eyes!

Leaning Tower of San 269 Martino

Nicknamed 'Campanile Storto' (crooked bell tower), it is a 16th century Roman Catholic church. The tower was unstable during its construction. In 1867, a bolt of lightning hit it, knocking off the angel topper. The soft ground made it lean further, forcing the city of Venice to take more stabilizing measures.

Bepi's House

Giuseppi Toselli, or Bepi Suà (Bepi of the Candies), used to hang a bed sheet over the side of his house and play outdoor movies for his neighbors. Later, he sold candies and sweets, giving him his nickname. This house is treasured on the island and is one of the more photographed homes in Burano.

Lego® House

One of the most pleasant afternoons you will spend while in Venice will be on this 52-acre island of cuteness. Burano has its own unique personality with sweetness pouring out of every door and window. Take the time to walk between the main streets and get to know the friendly people. You won't regret it. These colorful bricks resemble the Lego® toy blocks.

OUTER ISLANDS

LACE MUSEUM

OUTER ISLANDS

Over the centuries, the women of Burano spent so much time mending the fishnets of their husbands' boats that the skill was perfected, and the process became part of their local island culture. Sometimes competitions would ensue as the stitches became smaller and smaller; the complexities of the knots and techniques became tighter and tighter. The applications spread to other items such as tablecloths and garments. Their reputation spread far and wide, and soon orders were coming in from wealthy women all over Europe. The little community of Burano became famous for creating the most precious of lace products. Today as you walk through Burano, a visit to the Lace Museum will give you a strong sense of the personality of the community and of its local pride. Unfortunately, young women today are not learning this intricate art, and so it is fast becoming a piece of Burano's genuinely colorful history.

The Burano Lace Museum is easy to find in the Piazza Galuppi. All over town, you will find women creating lace goodies in many of the little shops. Stop and say 'hello' as they are happy to show your their work.

The museum is located at the historic palace of Podestà of Torcello, in Piazza Galuppi, Burano, seat of the famous Burano Lace School from 1872 to 1970. Rare and precious pieces offer a complete overview of the history and artistry of the Venetian laces, from its origins to the present day are on display, in a picturesque setting decorated in the typical colors of the island.

Wedding dresses created with stunning lace handiwork are a common order for the local Burano lace makers.

OUTER ISLANDS

TORCELLO

OUTER ISLANDS

Torcello *(tor-CHEH-lo)*, was the first island settled in the mid-400s as the more educated citizens of the mainland city of Altinum fled to the marshy islands to escape the Mongol burning of their city by Attila the Hun. Its residents quickly became proficient at utilizing the surrounding salt flats to mine and export salt. This in turn provided a stable economy, creating solid trading relationships throughout the mainland, parts of Western Europe, and countries to the East. Additionally, it established a strong political foundation as well.

In the 600s the Bishop of Altinum came to Torcello and erected the Church of Santa Maria Assunta. Still standing today, the mosaics inside the church are the most interesting site to see. Besides the astounding floor mosaic *(far-right)*, the piece in the Nave is brilliant: the Virgin Hodegetria stands out in a plain gold background with

Legend of The Devil's Bridge

During the 1800s Venice was ruled by the Austrians. Their soldiers were ever-present. A young Venetian girl, demonstrating her political incorrectness, fell in love with an Austrian soldier, much to the dismay of her family. Legend has it that her family had the boy murdered. The distraught girl hired a witch who told the girl to meet with her on the bridge of the secluded island of Torcello. The witch made the devil promise to bring the boy back to life, and in exchange, she promised the devil that she would bring him the soul of a recently deceased baby to him every Christmas Eve. But the old witch died. Each year on Christmas Eve, the devil, disguised as a black cat, mysteriously shows up at the bridge waiting in vain for the souls promised to him by the witch. Alas poor devil, they never appear.

From this Bell Tower   You Get This View!

Attila's Throne

This stone chair is said to be the Throne of Attila the Hun, the vicious marauder that invaded the mainland. However, other than a few ambitious strays, the Huns did not come to Torcello, nor did Attila use this chair to rule the locals. Instead, it has been used by local governors as they presided over local issues. The name and the legend remain useful today.

Hemingway's Island Muse

In 1948, Ernest Hemingway stayed on the Island of Torcello while he wrote the novel "Across the River and Into the Trees," using descriptive scenes of Torcello as the backdrop in the story.

the Saints. Near the door is a mosaic rendering of the Harrowing of Hell. Additionally, the depiction of Heaven demonstrates poignancy in its detail, while the the depiction of The Damned strikes fear in the heart of onlookers.

Torcello reached its cultural heights in the 11th century, boasting a population of over 10,000 citizens. Later, the arrival of the plague and the changing waters of the Lagoon forced her population to relocate to other islands. Over the centuries, the population of Torcello dwindled steadily to a trickle. The population of Torcello today occasionally rises above 10 residents that oversee the details of the island, but the general population is long gone.

VENICE

SAN FRANCESCO
Saint Francis of the Desert

Saint Francis of Assisi had spent time doing charitable works in Egypt. Upon his return to the Venice area in 1220, he searched for a place to rest, contemplate, and meditate. In the Venetian Lagoon near the island of Burano, there lay a quiet island. In antiquity, the island was inhabited by the Romans, but by the time Francis arrived, it was owned by Jacopo Michiel, a local Noble. When Francis first came to the island, the birds greeted him with their songs. This told Francis that he had found the perfect place for solace.

A couple of years later when Jacopo Michiel passed away, he donated the island to the Friars Minor to build a Church, the first ever to be dedicated to Saint Francis of Assisi. In the 1400s, the Church and the Convent were rebuilt, and to those they added the Cloister. The facility remained occupied by the Friars, until 1806 when Napoleon forced the Friars to move to the Convent of San Bonaventura.

Napoleon used the buildings to house a variety of munitions, recognizing that its thirty-one little cells would be ideal storage rooms. The rest of the facility served as a barracks for his troops.

Today you can hire a private boat to take you to Isla San Francesco del Deserto. Instead of a typical tour guide, one of the friendly Friars, for a small fee, will happily show you around the Monastery.

Away from the Crowds

If you are seeking a quiet place to escape the throngs that plague Venice, the island of San Francesco is just the place. Like Saint Francis of Assisi, you can stroll the gardens of the Church and listen to the birds to find your inner peace.

This is the narrow entrance to the Church of San Francesco del Deserto. Since public transportation is not available to this island, you must hire a small private boat to bring you across from the Island of Burano.

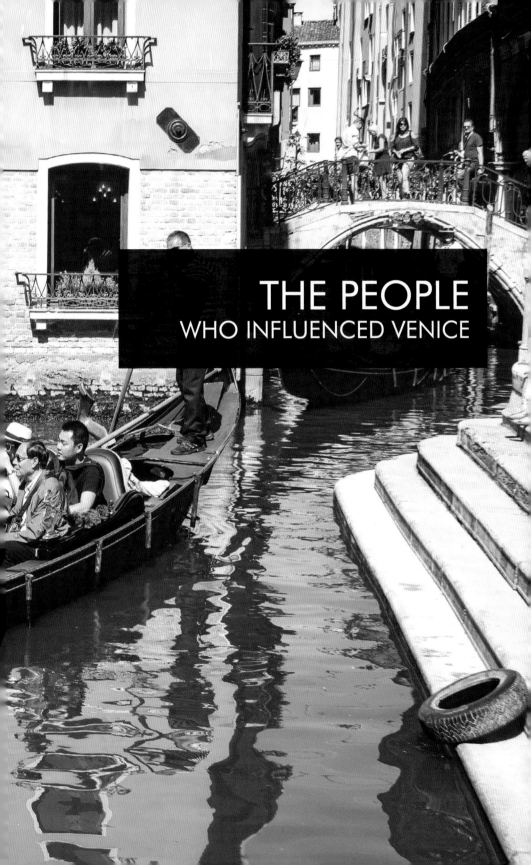

THE PEOPLE
WHO INFLUENCED VENICE

THE PEOPLE

THE PEOPLE (150)

150 THE PEOPLE

There were multitudes of people that have greatly influenced Venice, too many to name here. However, because Venice was an isolated city, many of those names remained local and did not achieve fame on a global basis. The following people have left their mark upon the pages of Venetian history, many of whom will leave their mark in your hearts as well.

200 Marco Polo
We all know Marco Polo as the guy that forged new trading paths from Europe to China. It was while he was imprisoned in Genoa that he met a writer who was happy to write about Polo's tales of travel. That's why we know him - because his stories were written down!

206 Gentile Bellini
Born in Venice to Jacopo Bellini, the brothers Bellini each grew to their own level of fame in the highly competitive arena of top Venetian Renaissance artists. Gentile was considered the more renowned of the two. As a painter, his work transformed the way art was seen, and his fame grew far and wide.

207 Giovanni Bellini
Giovanni became a true leader in Venetian Renaissance painting in his lifetime. Like his father, Giovanni enjoyed experimenting with oils, creating a line of deep rich colors that had not yet been seen. His use of bold color combined with gentle thematic images revolutionized artistic thinking.

208 Fra Luca Pacioli
A Monk, This versatile mathematical genius published several volumes about mathematics, chess, magic, and the first text book on accounting. A friend of Leonardo da Vinci, they influenced each others' work, and thinking.

Giorgione 210

Born in Castelfranco in the Venetian Republic as Giorgio Barbarelli da Castelfranco, little is known of Giorgione's brief but influential life. Local Venetians will describe him as 'handsome and amorous.' His paintings can be enjoyed all over the city of Venice.

Titian 212

Of all of the Venetian artists, Titian is arguably one of the true greats in the world of Renaissance painters. Some of his contemporaries were known to have called him "the Sun amidst small stars." His flexibility bordered on magic, because he was as comfortable painting landscapes, as religious stories, as portraits.

Tintoretto 216

Another of the true great Venetian painters, Tintoretto was known for the speed at which he could produce masterpieces and the boldness in his strokes. He was one of the most prolific painters of his day, as you will see his work proudly exhibited in many churches and museums all throughout the city.

Veronese 220

Paolo Verones's work was greatly influenced by Tintoretto. He enjoyed painting historical and religious stories utilizing over-sized spaces. Many of his large-format works have survived, and are exhibited all around Venice as well as in a variety of places around the world.

THE PEOPLE

222 Shakespeare

Surprisingly, little is known of Shakespeare's early life. He loved to read the stories of travel from other authors and playwrights, which is how he learned enough about Venice to write the famous plays that were set here: Othello, and The Merchant of Venice. Historians agree that he probably never actually set foot in Venice, however. But those plays make his spirit felt here.

224 Antonio Vivaldi

Best known for his sublime "Four Seasons," Antonio was born in Venice to a dad that was a famous violinist in St. Mark's Basilica. He became an ordained priest at age 25, but decided never to undertake his ecclesiastical responsibilities. Why? Music had a stronger voice in his head, giving him the direction that made him famous for centuries to come.

226 Tiepolo

Called a Master Decorator (a term used for artistic painters), Tiepolo was a prolific artist who enjoyed the use of bright colors in his work. Unlike the dark environs within Titian's or Tintoretto's work, Tiepolo's paintings were bright, well-lit, and sometimes even happy and light. Not only are his works found around Venice, but around the world including in many cities in the United States.

122 Carlo Goldoni

Goldoni was a delightful fellow with a sense of humor, that sometimes got him into trouble as a youth. His humor did not leave him as an adult, and his dreams included bringing humor onto the stage ~ instead of what he considered to be dry, old stories. He became equally famous in England as well as Italy, and Venice is proud to call him one of their own.

Casanova 228

You may already know a lot about Casanova's famous reputation with women. But did you know that he was from Venice? And that he was imprisoned for fornication? And that his prison sentence ended after a daring escape from the cells within the Doge's Palace?

Mozart 232

When he was 15 years old, Wolfgang made his second trip to Italy, including a one-month-long visit to Venice with his father and sister. He was known to have commented that he enjoyed his visits to Venice because this was a the best place to get the peace and quiet required for composing.

Richard Wagner 233

Richard Wagner is best known for his dramatic musical compositions, such as the "Ride of the Valkyries" and the "Flying Dutchman." The piece that has enhanced many a wedding aisle is his sublime "Bridal Chorus."

Napoleon Bonaparte 234

Napoleon had his sights set on the gem that was Venice. But how could such a force as Venice be conquered? A man gifted with a long-term strategic foresight, Napoleon noticed that Venice had created a flaw in its armor, and he was going to use it to conquer this beautiful gem!

Peggy Guggenheim 140

An early 20th century woman with a mind of her own, and family funds to pair with it, gained quite an ungainly reputation under the scrutiny of the media. Her collection in Venice is a sublime assortment of Modernism of the 1900s.

MARCO POLO - Explorer/Trader
1254 - 1324

Little Marco was born in the Republic of Venice in September of the year 1254, the son of Niccolo Polo a traveling merchant and his mother who died when Marco was a small child. It is commonly contested today whether Marco was born in Venice or in Croatia. However, back then, Croatia (known at the time as Dalmatia) was formally a part of the Republic of Venice, so it seems that both sides may be correct.

Marco Polo
mosaic by Salviati 1888

Niccolo and his two brothers were away on a trading mission in the far east when Marco was born. In fact, Niccolo did not even know that he had a son until returning home after traveling for 15 years, to learn that his wife had passed away and that he had a 15-year-old son.

Niccolo and his two brothers had intended to return years earlier, but they continually ran into issues throughout their journey. These included being treated so well by Kublai Khan that they decided to stay longer; being unsure of the temperament of a new ruler, they began the long journey home; roads were dangerous because of robbers or gangs; war in certain countries made passibility impossible, sometimes for years at a time; crossing bodies of water could be difficult because of pirates or war, etc.

Back home, our young Marco, being without a mother, lived with his grandmother. However, when his father returned home, Marco spent his days following the man all around and listening to his exciting stories of other cultures and people from faraway lands. He learned several languages, including Chinese dialects. He learned about life on the road, the ins and outs of trading, and some keen negotiating skills, as they differed from country to country.

By the time he was seventeen years old, Marco felt ready to join the men on their next foray to the mysterious lands in the east.

The Journey
Marco, Nicolo, and Uncle Maffeo set out on their journey with gifts and specialty items for Kublai Khan. At a fair pace of 5-8 miles per

THE PEOPLE

day, their trek took approximately four years to reach their destination.

Upon a warm greeting from his old friend Kublai Khan, Niccolo offered his son Marco in servitude. Khan relied on Marco for a number of tasks. As time passed, the talented young man showed a jubilant disposition and a good mind for numbers. Khan used him to roam the country to collect taxes and to gather information from the villages afar and bring this information back to Khan.

The visible presence of the Polos began to relax a general mistrust that the Chinese had for Westerners. People became used to seeing them around and enjoyed the idea of trading their trinkets for the unusual items from the West. On the other side, the Polos learned all they could from this strange society.

On cold nights, the Chinese burned a strange black stone to create heat for their homes and in their ovens for cooking. Marco thought it odd that when heated, the rock would turn a vivid red and stay hot for a long time. They learned that this 'coal' could easily be found in Europe, and that this was a great idea to bring back home - if indeed they ever found their way back to Venice.

Being professional merchants, one thing that the Polo men understood was money. However, the fact that the Chinese oddly used paper for money was a completely foreign concept to them. They knew only the value of gold and silver, of precious stones and pearls. But paper?
By order of the Khan, every town and village around China dealt with this paper form of money.

Paper Money?

~ Excerpted from the book
"Travels of Marco Polo"

In this city of Cambalu is the mint of the grand khan, who may truly be said to possess the secret of the alchemists, as he has the art of producing money by the following process. He causes bark to be stripped from those mulberry-trees the leaves of which are used for feeding silk-worms, and takes from it that thin inner ring which lies between the coarser bark and the wood of the tree. This being steeped, and afterwards pounded in a mortar, until reduced to a pulp, is made into paper, resembling that which is made from cotton, but quite black. When ready for use, he has it cut into pieces of money of different sizes, nearly square, but somewhat longer than they are wide.

MARCO POLO

Gone were the days of hauling around heavy bags and boxes of metal and stones. Paper money could be easily hidden from thieves. The age-old problem of arguing over the quality and grade of precious metals and stones to establish the value in a trade went away. Additionally, the complex way that it was manufactured made it nearly impossible to duplicate and established a uniformity throughout the land. This paper concept took awhile to grasp, but eventually they came to understand the usefulness of such a system.

The Ghost of a Chinese Princess

A local legend is told that Marco Polo fell in love with a daughter of Kublai Khan, married her, and brought her back home to Venice. His sisters, who lived with him, did not take a liking to this strange and quiet woman whom their brother had brought back from China. So when Marco Polo was arrested and imprisoned in Genoa, his sisters told their sister-in-law that he was killed. This so broke her heart that she gathered her clothes and threw them out of the window into the canal below. She immediately followed by throwing herself to her death below as well. Since then, people have reported seeing a white fog in Corte del Milion where they all lived in Canneregio. This fog is often accompanied by a faint woman's voice humming a strange Asian tune.

P.S. In recent years, construction crews were working on the theatre that is now in the place of his house, and they found under the foundation an ancient Asian tiara, an Imperial coat, and the bones of a woman clearly of Asian decent.

Meals were lavish and they learned to enjoy an odd beverage made from rice. They came to find that it was a carefully fermented liquid that had the welcome effects of inebriation, a wine of sorts.

The Polos enjoyed their lives in China, so long as they remained in Khan's favor, and that Khan remained in power. However, over time the strength of power began to shift. The uneasy Polos decided to plan for the long journey back home to Venice. They departed China with a relatively large party of escorts to help transport their goods

THE PEOPLE

back to Venice and to assist in their safety on the long road.
As they traveled back through China in a westerly direction, the
Great Khan had fallen ill, and it was presumed that he would die.
This weakened the social and political structure throughout the
land, causing several incidents for the Polo men during their crossing
which slowed their journey.

Proceeding through the Middle East, they would pass through local
battles and skirmishes that had a further slowing effect on their
journey. Closed passages and old roads overtaken by new enemies
meant they had to double-back at times to find new routes.

At one point, a major war in the Middle East halted their return by
two years. At another, 4,000 of their gold coins were seized by the
Turks, weakening their home-bound fortune.

In 1295, they and their still considerable wealth which had since
been converted to gem stones, finally arrived home in Venice proper.
They brought back messages, stories, and treasures for trade. They
were greeted enthusiastically. Twenty years had passed since their
departure.

Back Home ~ Off to Prison
Once back home, they were eager to trade their unique products
with everyone around Italy and the West. Soon, war broke out between Venice and Genoa, and Marco, now nearly forty years old, was arrested and imprisoned in a Genoese prison for being an activist on the side of Venice.

His buoyant personality and natural charm won over fellow prisoners and guards alike. It seemed that everyone wanted to hear more of his strange and elaborate stories about his time in the East.

Women would visit the prison to bring him specially prepared food, in exchange for more stories. Men would come with furnishings for his cell so that he could be com-

Wine Time
~ *Excerpt from the book*
"Travels of Marco Polo"
"The greater part of the inhabitants of the province of Cathay [now China] drink a sort of wine made from rice mixed with a variety of spices and drugs. This beverage, or wine as it may be termed, is so good and well flavoured that they do not wish for better. It is clear, bright, and pleasant to the taste, and being made exceptionally hot, has the quality of inebriating sooner than any other."

THE PEOPLE

MARCO POLO

fortable, as he related more accounts of his journeys to the foreign lands.

During his incarceration, one of his prison-mates was known to have written books and stories about his own past. To him, Marco dictated his many adventures during their mutual imprisonment. Eventually, they published the book "Marco Polo's Travels." *[Note: by "publishing," we mean editing and binding a single copy. The printing press would not be invented by Gutenberg for another two hundred years.]* One year after his release from prison, he met and married Donata Badoèr, twenty-five years his junior. Together they bore three children, and stayed married for the remaining twenty-four years of his life.

Marco Polo died in 1324. His body is entombed in the Chiesa di San Lorenzo in Venice where you can pay tribute to him today.

YOU DECIDE

Marco Polo's book quickly became popular and was purchased as fast as hand-printers could write them. His stories were told far and wide, but because only a limited number could be produced, they quickly disappeared into the dark fog of history.

His stories continued to be repeated, however, and continued to grow in splendor with each telling. It is from these that we today still know of the journeys of Marco Polo to the far East.

Many scholars throughout the centuries have scoffed at these tales, because of the lack of proof and accountability in them. Other scholars feel that for the most part, and given what we know today about the Far East and the Middle East, most of his tales rang with truth.

Most seem to agree that even though Marco Polo was neither the first nor the largest trader in his day, nor was he the first or the last to visit China and the Middle East, we would not know of his journeys if it were not for fact that he was the one that bothered to write it down.

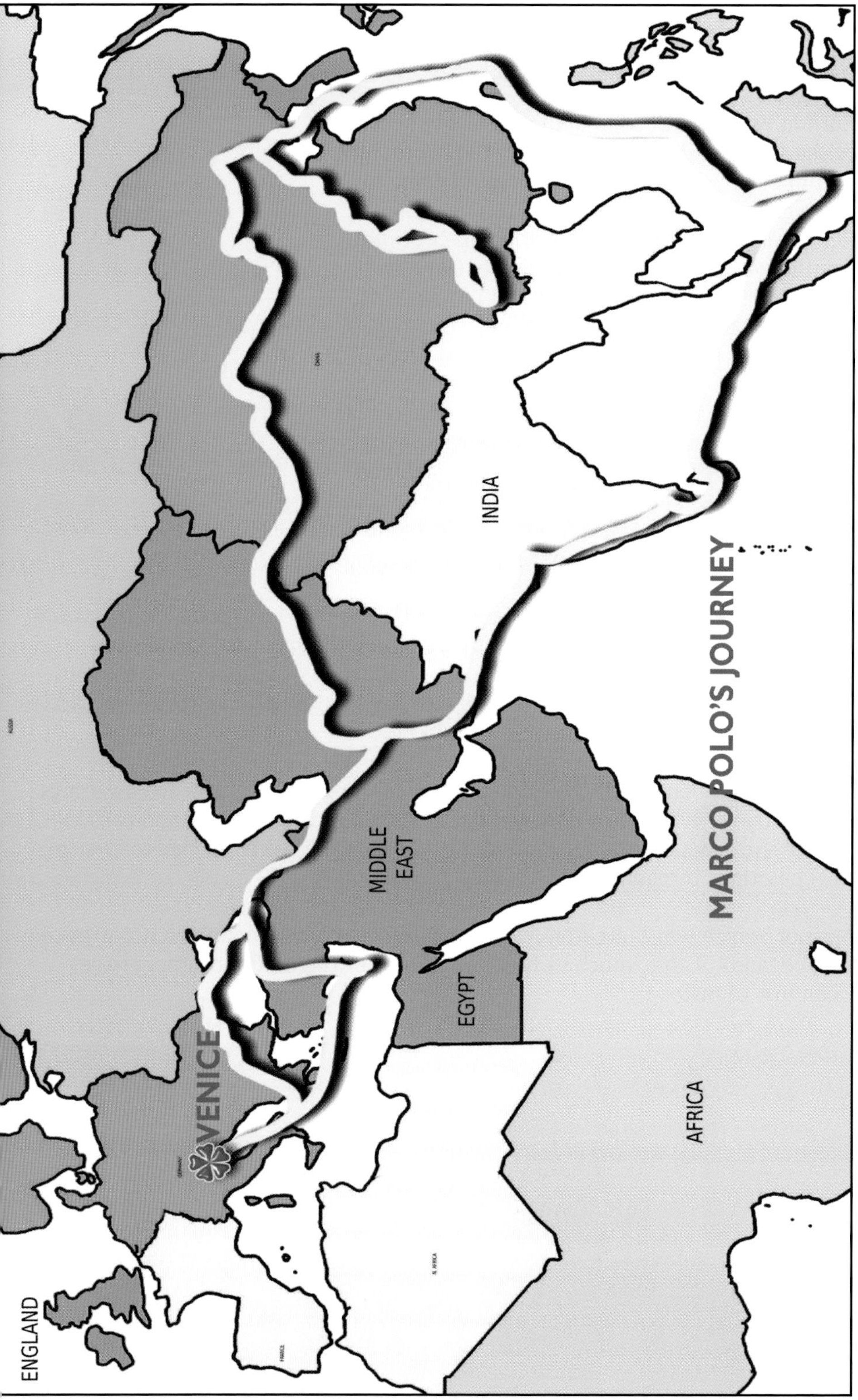

MARCO POLO'S JOURNEY

VENICE

ENGLAND

AFRICA

EGYPT

MIDDLE EAST

INDIA

GENTILE BELLINI - Artist
1429 - 1507

Born in Venice to Jacopo Bellini, a highly accomplished and influential oil painter, the brothers Bellini each grew to their own level of fame in the highly competitive arena of top Venetian Renaissance artists. In fact, during his lifetime, Gentile was considered the more renowned of the two. However, today, Giovanni has since stolen that crown from his slightly older brother.

Self-Portrait, 1496

As a measure of goodwill between Venice and the Turks, Gentile was sent to Constantinople as both a Good Will Ambassador and as an esteemed artist. There he painted his famed Sultan Mehmed II, the Scribe, and a variety of paintings that used new stylings that he learned while in Turkey. Upon his return, he became the official portraitist of the Doges for years to come.

Giovanni, on the other hand, became the true leader in Venetian Renaissance painting in his lifetime. Like his father Jacopo, Giovanni enjoyed experimenting with oils, creating a line of deep rich colors that had not yet been seen. His use of bold color combined with gentle thematic images revolutionized artistic thinking at that time.

From 1480 and on, Giovanni worked a job as the conservator of the paintings in the Doge's Palace. Not only was he to attend to the cleaning and preservation of the great artists before him, he also received commissions to create new paintings throughout the Palace.

Most of Venice was built from wood, making fires a commonplace occurrence. And because of this, much of the great works of the Bellini brothers have been lost to history.

"Sermon of St. Mark in Alexandria" an Oil on Canvas c.1504-7 by Gentile & Giovanni Bel

GIOVANNI BELLINI - Artist
1430 - 1516

Self-Portrait

"The Bellini"

This especially popular Venetian summer drink was named after our illustrious artistic family. Although there are variants to the recipe, it is made from peaches and Prosecco, an Italian sparkling wine. Served in a tall stemmed glass with either 2 ice cubes or blended with ice, its appeal comes from its ability to make one more tolerant of the summer heat of Venice.

"San Zaccaria Altarpiece" 1505
by Giovanni Bellini

St. Catherine

The Madonna holding the baby Jesus

Lucy, the Patron Saint of Sight

Saint Peter holding the Book of Heaven and the Key to the Gates

Angel playing a Violin

St. Jerome, the translator of the Bible

Upon entering the Church of San Zaccaria and approaching this piece, it becomes clear that Giovanni Belllini has almost invited you into this painting. Created in a niche, the figures in the painting seem so real, as though the action is truly unfolding right in front of you. His excellent use of perspective, light, and shadow bring a realness to the scene. This was indeed the mastery of Giovanni Bellini.

FRA LUCA PACIOLI - Mathematician
c.1447 - 1517

Born around 1447 in Sansepolcro, Italy, Luca became forever famous for this contributions in the area of mathematics.

At 18 years of age, he moved to Venice where he later became a Franciscan Monk. Over the decades, he tutored boys in arithmetic and published several books on the topic.

Near his 50th year, he was hired, in Milan by Duke Ludovico Sforza. While there, he met and befriended another of Sforza's 'team,' one by the name of Leonardo da Vinci. Together they taught and collaborated. For a period, they even lived together. That is, until Louis XII of France arrived, captured Milan and ousted Sforza, their mutual patron.

Like Dante's "Divine Comedy," Fra Pacioli's books were written in the vernacular (local dialect), rather than the formal Latin language. This opened mathematics up to less-educated young men who showed a knack for numbers, but who were not educated in Latin.

His book "The Divine Proportions" was largely illustrated by Leonardo, as was his treatise "On the Game of Chess". His Chess book, lost for centuries, was recently found in 2006 among a private collection.

Known as the Father of Modern Accounting, he wrote in detail, explaining the Double-Ledger system of accounting that was used throughout Italy at the time. This system has not changed in over 500 years and remains in practise today.

Additionally, he wrote a book about "Magic, the first book to explain card tricks. This book included instructions on fire-eating, juggling, and mathematics puzzles.

Pacioli died in Sansepolcro, where it is believed that he spent his final years.

Luca Pacioli, attributed to Jacopo de Barbari, c1460s

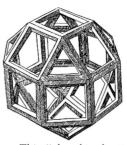

Above: *This "rhombicuboctahedron" was drawn by Leonardo da Vinci* **129***, to illustrate a topic in Pacioli's 1509 book "De divina proportione" ("Of Divine Proportions"), as discussed in the Vetruvian section of the book.* ***Below:*** *"Vetruvian Man" was designed by da Vinci to assist Pacioli in his discussions of Divine Proportions.*

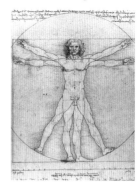

DEBITS

CREDITS

He who does nothing makes no mistakes; he who makes no mistakes learns nothing.

CHESS MAGIC

MATHEMATICS

GEOMETRY

FRA LUCA PACIOLI
Inventor of the Double-entry
bookkeeping system

"Each party in a business transaction will receive something and give something in return. In bookkeeping terms, what is received is a debit, and what is given is a credit."

This painting, attributed to Jacopo de Barbari **38**, illustrates Pacioli: his left hand resting on a book (his own?); his right hand creates a geometric figure on a palette with the name of Euclid. His famous multihedron dangles over the table that holds his mathematicians tools. The young man could be his student Durer, or simply a representation of the perpetual student.

GIORGIONE - Artist
1477 - 1510

THE PEOPLE

Born in Castelfranco in the Venetian Republic as Giorgio Barbarelli da Castelfranco, little is known of Giorgione's brief but influential life. 'Giorgione' translates to 'tall George' or 'Large George' implying that our young Giorgione was a big fellow. Local Venetians will describe him as 'handsome and amorous.'

Self-Portrait c.1510

From a young age, Giorgione apprenticed in the studio of Giovanni Bellini, which influenced much of Giorgione's works.

Among art historians, an air of mystery surrounds Giorgione and his paintings. This could be due to the fact that his topics were not traditionally expressed. For example, when commissioned to paint a typical religious story from the Bible, Giorgione would include realistic-looking backgrounds with bold, colorfully represented

Due to the ravages of history, we know of only five Giorgione paintings that have survived.

Young Man with an Arrow c. 1506

Boy with a Flute c. 1508

Three Philosophers c. 1509

Sleeping Venus c. 1510

scenes of nature. Traditional symbolic imagery seems to be absent in his works, and the scenes don't readily explain themselves.

The best example of this is in "The Tempest," the painting shown below. His use of color and his interest in 'sfumato' (likely obtained from a visit from Leonardo da Vinci, the master of sfumato, who had visited Venice around 1500) had landed him a permanent place in Venetian Renaissance art history.

In the early 1500s, a particularly nasty strain of the Plague passed through Italy, hitting Venice quite hard. The newly-famous artist Giorgione fell victim, and succumbed in 1510 at the age of 33.

THE TEMPEST
c. 1508, is the most famous of Giorgione's five remaining paintings.

THE PEOPLE

TITIAN - Artist
1488(?) - 1576

Tiziano Vecellio *(pron: teet-zee-AH-no veh-CHEH-lee-oh, TEE-shun)* was born during the High Renaissance period (1450 - 1525) in a small town in the Dolomite mountain range called Pieve di Cadore. He came from a family of notable politicians as well as artists.

As a boy, he was sent to apprentice at the school of Sebastiano Zuccati to become a mosaicist. He was later moved to the school of the genuinely famous artist Gentile Bellini whose family enjoyed master fame in the world of Venetian art. Shortly thereafter, young Tiziano moved under another master of the Bellini family, Giovanni Bellini. And it was there that Tiziano - later known as Titian - solidified his own style which he enjoyed fame and notoriety for life.

While under the Bellini tutelage, Titian befriended another artist who's work he had long admired. This was the already renowned Giorgio Barbarelli da Castelfranco, who went by the name of Giorgione. The two often collaborated on paintings and projects, which has led experts to quarrel over which painting was painted by which artist. Nevertheless, both artists grew stylistically and personally from their collaboration and friendship.

> Titian was known to have good-naturedly said that "Good painters really only need three colors: black, white, and red."

At the age of 37, Titian married Cecilia who had already borne him a son. After their marriage, Cecilia gave birth to one more son and two daughters. Sadly, his beloved Cecilia died while giving birth to their second daughter.

After the death of his wife, a stylistic change became apparent. He departed from the bold deep colors for which he became famous, to more muted, blended colors.

Titian died a victim of the Black Plague 1576, but because of the unknown year of his birth, he could have been anywhere between 85 and 100 years old at his death. His body is interred in Santa Maria Gloriosa dei Frari, in Venice.

Soon after Titian died, his son and only heir Orazio also fell victim to the Plague. As Titian left no formal will, the disbursement of his estate became a complicated affair of its own, as many entities stepped forward with a claim to his fortune, valid or not.

"Pesaro Madonna"
Seen today in Santa Maria Gloriosa dei Frari, in Venice

THE PEOPLE

St. Peter referring to his great book of names.

Titian used his wife Cecilia as the model for the Madonna.

The Baby Jesus is captivated by St. Francis

The Olive Leaves represent peace, unity.

St. Francis of Assisi leads the Pesaro family in an introduction to the Madonna.

The Papal Coat of Arms is represented on the banner.

Jacopo Pesaro is the Patron of this painting.

The Pesaro family witness the judgement of Jacopo Pesaro.

St. Peter's Key to the Gates of Heaven has fallen to the steps, alluding to the idea that this is the stairway to heaven.

What do you see?
This is a superb example of Titian's unique blending of the pyramidal high renaissance style with a shifting of placement of the key figure away from being the center point of a painting. Here the key figure of the Madonna has been placed off to the right, making it ideal for the passers-by in the Frari to view it on their way up to the Altar. The most striking element of this painting is Titian's use of bold, well-defined colors that beautifully offset each other within the canvas as a whole.

213

THE PEOPLE

Symbolism as a Language

Since the Classical period, symbolism was widely used in every form of art as a 'language' to communicate the meaning of a piece. There are a variety of reasons for this: understanding a piece of work is simple, even if literacy were low; fashion dictates; hidden meanings might represent a code or message that only a specific audience was intended to understand. When pieces are discovered with no obvious symbolism, historians often show befuddlement.

"The Assumption" was created when Titian was in his late 20's. This 23-foot tall mega painting is in the main Apse inside Santa Maria Gloriosa dei Frari.

Light and Oil

The strength of trade with the Far and Middle East gave Venice an advantage with colors and mediums. Trade brought minerals and powders rich of color that would enable the artist to create levels of boldness and subtlety that Renaissance artists in other cities lacked. In addition, when mixed with oils, these colors carried elements of translucence and reflectivity that made the artists (and their patrons) crave more. In a competitive effort to master light and reflection in his works, Titian was known to have added ground up glass to his paintings.

King of the Lagoon

During his earlier years, Titian, Giorgione, and Bellini were the Triad of power amongst the great Venetian artists. However, when Giorgione and Bellini each passed away, this left Titian to hold the title as the greatest artist in Venice for the next 60 years!

The Mysteries of
"The Sacred and the Profane"
Titian, c. 1514, Oil on canvas. Galleria Borghese, Rome

This piece, which can be found in the Borghese Gallery in Rome, has been clouded in mystery and speculation since its conception in the 1600s. Its lack of obvious symbolism has caused art historians to argue amongst themselves as to the intent of the artist. It appears that a bride sits upon a Roman sarcophagus. Venus, shrouded in a red cloth, sits on the other side with Cupid playing in the water, occupying the center space. A walled village rises behind the bride, while a village with a church tower are behind Venus. Hunters chase a jack rabbit and a shepherd tends to a flock of un-standing (dead? sleeping?) sheep. Rabbits, typically symbolizing lust, are throughout.

The piece was commissioned by a secretary to the Venetian Council of Ten, Niccolò Aurelio. This is denoted by his family coat of arms on the sarcophagus. Right next to that, is a phallic-looking water spout with water pouring forth. This is said to to represent Aurelio himself. The placement of the Coat of Arms and the spout between the women should also have meaning. It cannot be agreed upon as to the identity of the women: some believe they are his bride and Venus; some feel that these are the bride's two sides of both a Virgin and a Lusty, more Earthy woman. So what about those opposing villages behind them? All those rabbits? The smoking incense burner? What does the water symbolize? What about the figures on the front of the sarcophagus?

As you can see, this painting has mystified and irritated its viewers for over 500 years. What do you see?

FINDING TITIAN

~ Santa Maria Glorioso dei Frari

~ Santa Maria della Salute

~ Scuola di San Rocco

~ Ca' D'Oro

~ Palazzo Ducale

~ Gallerie dell'Accademia

~ San Giovanni Elemosinario

~ Gesuiti

~ San Salvador

~ San Sebastiano

~ Biblioteca Nazionale Marciana

~ Museo Correr

~ Rome & Global

TINTORETTO - Artist
1518(?) - 1594

THE PEOPLE

Born Jacomo Robusti in the Canareggio district of Venice, Tintoretto showed natural abilities with his use of dyes and colors at a young age. His mother tried to dissuade young Jacomo from heading toward the arts. His father, a well-known dyer (tintore), encouraged the young lad to experiment more with colors and mediums.

Being that this was the age of the Protestant Reformation, Tintoretto became a religious painter with skills and insights that have never before been seen in the art world.

Self-portrait, Circa 1546-1548. Oil on canvas. Philadelphia Museum of Art

Throughout his youth, his idol was Titian, who held the 'crown' as the most revered artist in Venice. Titian, always on the lookout for a young upstart that could possibly begin stealing his spotlight, noticed young Jacomo - Tintoretto early on.

The Little Dyer

Tintoretto's father, Giovanni Battista, was a dyer, also known as a tinter. 'Tintoretto' literally means little dyer because as a child, he too enjoyed playing with colors. And too, when full grown, he was approximately 5-feet tall. Hence the name Tintoretto or Little Dyer stuck with him.

When he was around 21 years old, Venice was considered to be one of the most cosmopolitan cities in Europe. Tintoretto created his first signed work, "Sacra Conversazione," which he signed as Jachobus. His career was taking off.

One of his favorite places to 'decorate' was the little church of Santa Maria dell Orte, as it was the church since boyhood, and it was a mereone-minute walk around the corner from his lifelong home.

Throughout his lifetime, he produced more than 650 great works of art that can be found all around the city of Venice as well as the world.

The single most revered event in the history of Venice is the story that in the 800s, a group of Venetian merchants went down to (Islamic) Alexandria, Egypt, to find the body of St. Mark and bring it back to Christian Venice. After doing so, they built the St. Mark's Cathedral in his honor.

• •

Tintoretto's "Abduction of San Marco" can be found in the Gallerie dell'Accademia.

Stealing the body of Saint Mark by Tintoretto

This is a trademark example of Tintoretto's style. His masterful use of perspective boldly defies the orderliness of typical Renaissance styles. The dead body of St. Mark is foreshortened; and his use of limited color, varying light, and off-shooting perspective create the mood of disjointed chaos that is happening on the right.

THE PEOPLE

TINTORETTO

Having created a over 650 masterpieces, Tintoretto left our world, but not without having changed and influenced the art world forever.

In 1594, he was gripped with crippling stomach pains and fever which lasted a couple of weeks before he passed on. He is entombed in his home church of Santa Maria dell'Orto. Next to him, lies the body of his daughter Marietta who died four years earlier at the young age of 30.

Self-portrait, 1588. Oil on canvas. Paris, Louvre

Left - This was Tintoretto's home for his entire life. Each day he would walk the few short steps around the corner to the church of Santa Maria dell'Orto - right. Today you can walk these same few steps to enjoy the Tintoretto-filled interior and to pay your respects to his tomb during your visit.

Foreshortening

Foreshortening is a technique of perspective used when painting or drawing someone that is not facing the audience head-on. In this example, if this man on the beach were to stand up, he would be taller than the space within the canvas would allow. In order to paint the man laying down, he would have to be fore-shortened to produce the correct angle.

Tintoretto, a master of foreshortening, was known to suspend his models from the ceiling beams so that he could walk below them, and looking up, he could find the correct perspective needed to foreshorten a person to a laying-down position in his paintings.

Below left - The Scuola Grande di San Rocco is a must-see for Tintoretto fans and foes alike. Decorated from ceiling to basement by Tintoretto, this is the best place in the city to truly appreciate his works.

Finding Tintoretto
~ Church of Madonna del Orto
~ Scuola Grande di San Marco
~ Scuola Grande di San Rocco
~ Church of San Rocco
~ Palazzo Ducale
~ Gallerie dell'Accademia, Venice
~ Santa Maria del Giglio, Venice
~ Santa Maria del Rosario
~ Santa Maria della Salute
~ San Zaccaria
~ San Cassiano
~ Santo Stefano
~ San Polo
~ San Trovaso
Tintoretto's works can also be found in dozens of cities spread throughout the world.

THE PEOPLE

PAOLO VERONESE - Artist
1528 - 1588

Born the fifth child in his family as Paolo Spezapreda in the Venice township of Verona, Paulo was given his sir name from his father's profession as a stone cutter, or spezapreda. He eventually took his mother's maiden name, as she (illegitimately) possessed a Noble lineage. When he moved to Venice, however, he decided to call himself after his hometown of Verona, hence, Veronese (pron veh-ro-NAY-seh).

By the age of 13, he was apprenticing with Antonio Badile and Giovanni Francesco Caroto, both of whom were considered to be Masters during the Venetian Renaissance period. By the time he was 18, he had already surpassed his teachers and chose to move on.

Self-portrait, oil on canvas.
c.1558-1563.
Hermitage Museum,
Saint Petersburg, Russia

Veronese's specialty was people, which he called 'figures.' He seemed to enjoy painting large scenes decorated with many types of people busy doing everyday things. His scenes typically represent a complicated and rollicking good time, as though everyone in them is celebrating something. Coupled with his taste for bold vibrant colors of a wide variety, his scenes seemed to cheer every room in which they hung.

"Veronese paints the happiest paintings in the world!"
~The Guardian, March 2014

His style was a clear departure from the more staid form of mannerism with which he was trained, leading to a long line of commissions for his super large, hyper-jovial scenes. It appears that even though most of his commissions came from the Church, Veronese seemed less concerned with adhering to traditional illustration of Biblical scenes, as he was with transforming them into events that occurred during his modern time, in his modern Venice. It is this for which he is remembered.

Veronese was visiting his summer home in Sant' Angelo where he managed to catch a pulmonary virus, such as bronchitis or pneumonia. He is entombed in Venice, in his childhood Church of San Sebastiano ~ the place where he spent a huge amount of his time in decoration.

Veronese's home on the Salizzada San Samuele

THE PEOPLE

"The Last Supper" commissioned in 1573 by the Convent of Sts. Giovanni e Paolo, now entitled "Feast in the House of Levi"

urban 'earers — *Man with Toothpick* — *Buffoon with a Parrot* — *Striking Boy* — *Cat* — *Dog* — *Modern Clothing* — *Germans with Halberds*

In 1573, Paolo Veronese was summoned to answer for this 'anti-Christian' abomination, The Last Supper (above). Here is a paraphrase of the Inquiry:
  "Why are people wearing modern clothing? Turbans? Why are there German Soldiers with Halberds? What's with the Buffoon with a Parrot on his wrist? Is that boy going to strike him? What about the guy with the toothpick? And the cat under the table? And the dog in the front? Perhaps you should replace it with Mary Magdalene" they added.
  "Well, your Honors, I was commissioned to decorate the painting as I saw fit. And I saw fit to add all of these figures to it, because that's what I do," Veronese answered. In the end, Veronese changed nothing, except the name. This changed it from being an accurate Holy depiction to a scene of a typical banquet taking place during their current times.
NOTE: This painting can also be found under the name of "Christ in the House of Levi."

> "We painters take the same license that Poets and Jesters take."
> ~Veronese, during the Inquisition of 1573

Finding Veronese

~ Gallerie dell'Accademia, Venice
~ Palazzo Ducale (Doge's Palace)
~ Church of San Sebastiano
~ Saint Pantalon
Globally
Hundreds of works by Veronese are scattered around the globe. They can be found at the Louvre, at the Getty (Los Angeles, USA), at the Hermitage (Russia), and many other places.

SHAKESPEARE in VENICE
1564 - 1616

THE PEOPLE

Given his international notoriety over the centuries, it is interesting that few facts of his life have not necessarily been agreed upon, even today.

William was probably born in 1564, a date drawn from a baptismal record - not a birth record, in Stratford-upon-Avon, England. His actual date of birth may have been April 23, but again, this is not known for sure. Many like this date because it coincides with his death date of April 23, 1616 creating a fitting poetic symmetry. He was the 8th child of John & Mary Shakespeare, and he may have been educated at the King's New School in Stratford. He married Anne Hathaway at age

William Shakespeare Portrait
~ Katie Jones 2017

26, who, six months later, gave birth to a possibly illegitimately-conceived daughter. Three years later, they had twins, one of whom died at age 11. Even though his plays were set all over Europe, biographers are pretty sure that William never left England, and that he acquired his knowledge of Venice (and other foreign cities) from others who had traveled abroad, ie, the Earl of Oxford.

Over the years, William penned 37 plays, 154 sonnets, and 5 poems. Of the 37 plays: 13 were set in Italy, and of those, 2 were set in Venice: Othello and The Merchant of Venice. Because these were two of his more successful pieces, people have flocked to Venice in pursuit of finding the traces of the Moor, Othello, and his delicate wife, Desdemona.

Palazetto Contarini-Fasan
Possible home of
Shakespeare's Desdemona
of "Othello." Own works of
Nino Barbieri 2004

Asking Directions, the Shakespearean Way
Othello: Act 2, Scene 2

When Old Gobbo asks: "Master young gentleman, I pray you, which is the way to master Jew's?"

Launcelot replies: "Turn up on your right hand at the next turning, but, at the next turning of all, on your left; marry, at the very next turning, turn of no hand, but turn down indirectly to the Jew's house.

This is a perfect description of one's attempt to move through Venice using instructions - even today. You WILL get lost. Welcome to Venice!

Visitors have often mistaken this sculpture of a Moor as that of Othello. Standing on a street-corner in Canneregio, this Moor is actually one of the brothers Mastelli from Greece who was turned to stone because of his greedy ways.

During the time of Shakespeare's life, Venice had acquired an interesting reputation throughout Europe as being a city of lavish parties, over-indulgences, and steamy sexual affairs that could curl one's toes.

This is the perfect backdrop for Shakespeare's ilk of storyline where drama so masterfully intertwines with the daily lives of the rich and indulgent that people love to read about.

Venice is described in such opulent detail at every step that the city had clearly become a character of its own in both "Othello" as well as in "The Merchant of Venice."

"What news on the Rialto?" ~ Othello

Shakespeare included several scenes of the Rialto Market, a place where neighbors would converse and gossip daily; his character Shylock lived in the Jewish Ghetto in Cannaregio, the only place in Europe (at the time) where Jews could live and work openly.

Shakespeare fans love to come to Venice in search of the locations in his stories and to seek evidence of their actual existence.

ANTONIO VIVALDI
1678 - 1741

THE PEOPLE

Born in Venice, his father Giovanni Battista Vivaldi, a well-known violinist in St. Mark's Basilica, was Antonio's primary music teacher during his childhood. He took to music early and naturally. He was especially proficient with the violin, as chronic shortness-of-breath issues kept him from progressing very far with wind instruments.

He began studying for the priesthood at 15 years of age, and was ordained at 25. By then, however, music filled his head to such an extent that he never accepted his

Antonio Vivaldi, by an unknown artist

ecclesiastical duties. Nevertheless, he acquired the name of "il Prete Rosso," the Red Priest - due to the color of his hair.

Young Antonio found employment at the Ospidale della Pietà, the Devout Hospital of Mercy in Venice. This was an orphange, where the boys were taught skills, and girls were taught music. He instructed the girls in every aspect of music, including professional performance techniques.

His all-girl orchestra practiced and played his compositions, and were popularly requested to perform around the city and elsewhere. Vivaldi's fame as an accomplished and 'daring' Baroque composer had spread around Europe.

When he was in his thirties, a publisher from Amsterdam published his works under the name L'estro Armonico - Harmonic Inspiration. A well-known contemporary of Vivaldi's, a fellow by the name of Johann Sebastian Bach, acquired some of Vivaldi's pieces, and was so enamored with them that he played and performed them as well.

Vivaldi enjoyed a life of comfort, often accepting gigs in other cities. One such job landed him in the city of Mantua (approx 50 miles west of Venice), and while there he composed his beloved "Four Seasons."

Later in his life, the popular flavor of music began to transition from the highly-decorated, ornately-styled, polyphonic Baroque music to the more staid, homophonic, melody-driven Classical movement.

Even though Vivaldi was used to being requested by the top-most of royalty, and had access to the best musicians in Europe, these requests began to fall off. This had serious impacts on his financial stability.

To his further distress, rumors and accusations spread about his having an affair with one of his young students. This killed the remainder of his high-end performance requests.

Remembering his reliable friendship with the Holy Roman Emperor Charles VI in Austria, Vivaldi went there with the hopes that Charles would hire him. But soon after Vivaldi's arrival, Charles died, leaving Vivaldi with no patron, ergo, no income prospects.

Antonio died a pauper within a year after Charles' death, and was buried in Vienna in an unmarked grave.

Alas, no music was performed at his burial.

Visiting Vivaldi

Vivaldi fans may be interested in visiting the places throughout Venice where Vivaldi lived, worked, ate, prayed, etc. Unfortunately, so many of his places no longer exist. The church where he was baptized, the church where he grew up, his family home, the orphanage where he spent decades, all gone. Remaining is the Basilica di San Marco where he and his father performed.

THE PEOPLE

VENICE

TIEPOLO, Artist
1696 - 1770

Born Giovanni Battista Tiepolo in Venice, his name was blended to Giambattista Tiepolo. Little is known of his childhood and teen years; only that which was mentioned in the biography of his teacher Lazzarini.

While in his early twenties, his reputation swelled making him quite enviable among the favored artists in Venice.

Unlike many singularly-minded artists, Tiepolo was inspired by a wide variety of subjects throughout his life which is apparent in his works: Religion, Mythology, and History (see next page) occupied his mind, as did literary themes and allegorical works.

Giambattista Tiepolo self-portrait, from the Staircase of the Würzburg Residenzschloss

His styles varied throughout the years as well. As you can see from the three paintings on the right, he fluctuated between the darkness of tenebrism, to a lighter more ethereal style, to the detailed style of classicism.

His wife Cecilia, the sister of the Venetian artist Francesco Guardi, bore him ten children, seven of whom survived: four girls and three boys. Two of his sons flourished in their father's world of art and were known to accompany him when he was hired to paint royal homes in Germany, Spain, and others abroad. The Tiepolo family brought Venetian painting to new heights during the Rococo period, always with Giambattista at the helm.

By the time he reached his Senior years, the flavor for dramatic allegorical and religious paintings had dimmed, but his ability to produce a wide variety of styles and tastes kept him hugely popular until his death at age 74.

Tiepolo's works are cherished all around the world in museums small and large.

Finding Tiepolo

Tiepolo's incomparable works are spread throughout the world.

In Venice:
San Stae
Gallerie dell'Accademia
Palazzo Sandi
Sta Maria delle Consolazione
Scuola Grande di San Rocco
Basilica di San Marco
SantAlvise
Santi Apostoli
Scuola Grande dei Carmini
Doge's Palace
Fondazione Querini Stampalia

Globally:
Hermitage, St. Petersberg
Met Museum, NYC
Louvre, Paris
Prado, Madrid
National Gal of Art, Wsh DC
National Gallery, London

- Tiepolo's "Nativity," Oil on
- canvas, c. 1732. This is an
- example of Tiepolo using tene-
- brism in a traditional 'Nativity'
- scene. The focus of dark colors
- over light is representative of
- the tenebristic style. This had
- been hugely popular all over
- Europe for over a century, back
- to the famous dark styles pro-
- duced by Rembrandt. Here, Tie-
- polo has taken it to new heights
- as he uses the brightest light for
- the baby Jesus. Find this paint-
- ing in St. Mark's Basilica.

"Triumph of Zephyr and Flora"
Oil on Canvas, c. 1734-35.
Tiepolo brings together the God
of the Wind and the Goddess of
All that Blooms in his own Allegory of Spring. Notice his use
of lighter, even brighter colors,
and the gossamer dragonfly-like
wings of Zephyr. Several Puties
accompany them on their journey into a new season.

This painting can be found in
Venice, inside of Ca'Rezzonico's
museum of the 1700s.

"The Banquet of Cleopatra"
Oil on Canvas, c. 1744
Here Tiepolo dipped his brush
into a more classical palette
to depict one of his favorite
stories. It seems that Cleopatra
and Mark Antony of Rome,
participated in a wager to see
which of them could provide the
most expensive feast. Cleopatra
won the bet. Tiepolo's brilliance
at a more classical style is
apparent here. This painting is
hanging in the National Gallery
in Melbourne, Australia.

CASANOVA - Lothario
1725 - 1798

Giacomo Girolamo Casanova de Seingalt was born in Venice, the first of six children, to two stage performers. Our little Giocomo proved to be extremely bright and precocious even as a child.

Growing up in the San Samuele area of the San Marco Sestiere, he possessed an early thirst for learning, and so undertook as many classes as he could handle. He absorbed knowledge as easily as a silk kerchief in a new rain.

In his late teens, he began Seminary School, looking toward a life of Priesthood. However, unable even in youth to squelch his natural gravitation toward women, he was expelled.

Throughout his life, he was able to take on a wide variety of jobs as a stone mason, a violinist, an occulist, alchemist, and a magician. Additionally, he attended law school at the behest of a local benefactor, an endeavor much to his personal disdain. He studied medicine feeling that had he been luckier in life, he could have been a physician.

All the while, he honed his skills at the ability to coax, cajole, and connive. He was able to garner free food and rent from merchants and landlords; jobs from business owners; and party invitations from politicians. All the while, he was using these same expertly honed skills to expertly seduce all of their wives.

This ability, which he perfected to a 'T' worked so well, that it became his means for making his living. Many of the men in the community actually looked the other way when he pulled some of his cons, because he was actually making their wives happy.

His behavior soon came to an abrupt end when he was arrested for the charges of witchcraft. These charges may have stemmed from a jilted husband who also happened to be a powerful member of the community. The Inquisitors were brought from Rome (where even there Casanova's reputation festered in many men's craws) where they, without trial, convicted and confined him to the Leads prison in Venice.

After his masterful escape, he fled in the night to France where he changed his name to Jacques Casanova, the Chevalier de Seingalt, and won a small fortune in the lottery. Using his winnings, he continued to travel about Europe, and eventually returned to Venice, as a spy for the Venetian State Inquisitors.

Almost entirely forgotten in his later years, he wrote a book of his exploits and adventures, making him and his lotharious reputation famous for centuries to come.

THE PEOPLE

> "I have loved women even to madness, but I have always loved liberty better." ~ *Giacomo Casanova*

Venice in the 1700s

Venice enjoyed the luxuries of the center stage, being the pleasure capital of all of Europe. It was considered to be somewhat of the "Las Vegas" of the wealthy and was on the main tourist paths coming from every direction including London, Madrid, Paris, Austria, and Rome.

Both the Clergy as well as the local government not only tolerated the bending of social mores, but seemingly relished in the partaking of this lifestyle as well.

During the 1700's, it was stylish to wear a mask. This aided in the anonymous performance of rude and lascivious behavior.

> "The girl pleased me at once, though I had no idea why. It was she who little by little kindled in my heart the first sparks of a feeling which later became my ruling passion."
> ~ *Giacomo Casanova*

In the light of day, Venice looked as buttoned-up and well-behaved as most other major European cities. But when the sun went down, people would don their masks, wigs, hats and capes, to cavort and frolic about the city. Most behaviors were tolerated so long as people were not being harmed. Once your costume was donned, you could roam the streets and pubs in search of pleasures of your choice, all from the socially accepted disguise.

> "Is love anything else than a kind of curiosity? I think not; and what makes me certain is that when the curiosity is satisfied the love disappears." ~ *Giacomo Casanova*

Parties were common, and the Venice Carnivale became world famous for the no-holds-barred environment of huge wild parties and the throngs of party-goers that attended them regularly.

This was the perfect environment for one with a 'Casanovan' disposition to grow and thrive.

Casanova

An Angel of a Jailbreak

When he was 30 years old, Casanova's unrepentant ways got him arrested for lewdness and indecency. On July 26th of 1755, the Inquisition sentenced him (without a trial) to 5 years in the Leads prison. The Leads was aptly named for the fact that the building used lead panels to line its roof. The Leads prison was within the walls of the Doge's Palace, and Casanova's prison cell was a only one floor above the Inquisitor's Hall.

Of course, once in his cell, he began to ponder ways to escape. It was clear that even if he managed to escape his cell, he did not know how to leave the building without going through the two known passageways: the front door and the Bridge of Sighs.

> "I should have been allowed to do as I wished and become a physician, in which profession quackery is even more effective than it is in legal practice."

His cell was a tiny room with no furniture, except an armchair. This was a helpful piece of furniture, because as he stood at 6 feet 2 inches in bare feet, he was nearly 6 inches taller than the ceiling of his cell when standing. So he spent much of his sitting. Eventually, he was rewarded with a wooden plank for a bed.

He was allowed periodically to stretch his legs by walking in the attic which runs the length of the building. One day during one of these walks, he found some boxes. His natural curiosity led him to examine the contents of the boxes, where he soon found a piece of marble. He hid it within his clothes and took it back to his cell. During another such foray, he found an 18-inch-long metal bar. This too he hid in his clothing and returned to his cell.

Over time, he had used the piece of marble to file the end of the bar into a point - a shiv, if you will. When not in use, it lived in the arm of his chair. Now, what to do next? Breaking through the door would put him into a face-to-face confrontation with the guards, which he knew he could not win. Because, after all, Casanova was a lover, not a fighter.

Instead, he devised a different plan: he would simply dig through the floor of his cell to the office below. He would tear his sheets into strips, tie them together and use them as a rope to lower himself to the floor. He would then hide under a desk until someone came to open the office. Using his shiv for protection, he would run like the wind. Ok, this would be the perfect plan.

Each day, Casanova dug into the floor of his cell, layer by layer, and each night he would cover the hole with his bed. Nearing the end of his project, he was dreaming about his soon-to-be-found freedom, when the prison administration decided to gift him with a roommate. This fellow was then

I laughed and said, "I wonder how you derive your right to beat a free woman anywhere." Cassnova to Sr.Torriano after stopping the latter from mercilessly beating a young widow with a stick. ~ *Giacomo Casanova*

removed after only one week.
Knowing that the room below would be empty on the coming Wednesday, he waited anxiously for the days to pass.

Meanwhile, his friend and lawyer, Count Bragadin, who had been arguing appeals on behalf of Casanova, finally received a tiny concession for his client: Casanova would be moved to a larger cell.

His hopes dashed to pieces, Casanova found no choice but to devise another plan. After befriending a priest, Father Balbi, the Angel in the next cell, they together worked this new plan.

Realizing that his 'shiv' was moved inside the chair with him to his new cell, he tucked it inside a Bible and asked the guard to bring it along with his bowl of spaghetti to the nice priest next door. Balbi dug a hole in the ceiling of this own cell, climbed into the attic above, then proceeded to dig a hole down into Casanova's cell.

It was a dark and foggy night when they both climbed up to the attic, pried the lead panels loose from the ceiling, and climbed to the rooftop outside. Using bedsheets, they lowered themselves to a floor below, broke a window, and entered a large room, where they slept until dawn.

Upon waking, they left the room and walked the halls until they met with a guard. They explained that they had been accidentally locked in a room all night, whereby the guard was happy to unlock the large door. Casanova and Bilbo happily walked right out the front door where they had a cup of coffee in Saint Mark's Square, then parted ways.

From there, Casanova fled to France where he began a whole new chapter of his life.

MOZART - Composer
1756 - 1791

Born in Salzburg, Austria in 1756, a young Mozart visited Italy on three separate occasions with his father Leopold. Wolfgang was the youngest of seven children; five of whom died as babies. He and his sister Nannerl (née Anna Marie) were quite close as children, and often performed in recitals together.

When he was 15 years old, Wolfgang made his second trip to Italy, including a one-month-long visit to Venice with his father and sister. He was known to have comment-

A portrait of Mozart, aged 14, in Verona, 1770, by Saverio dalla Rosa

A plaque on the wall of the house where Mozart stayed during his brief visit to Venice:

"The 15 year old Wolfgang Amadeus Mozart stayed with friends in this house during the 1771 Carnival. The city of Vivaldi and Goldoni wants to remember the young man from Salzburg in whom the grace of musical genius combined with seventeenth century civility to create the most sublime poetry."

ed that he enjoyed his visits to Venice because it is truly the most serene place to be when you want peace of mind ~ La Serenissima!

The House

For centuries, it was unknown where he stayed during his visit to Venice. Research was done in the 1990s that proved where it was. In a letter written by Wolfgang, he wrote that he was staying in Casa Cavalletti. Because he was attempting to translate from Venetian to his own German, he misspelled (or misinterpreted) Ca' Falletti. As it turned out, Count Francesco Falletti Castelman had a rather unscrupulous reputation of using the house as a brothel (among other things) and was sentenced to death. Nevertheless, it is said that he was the inspiration for Mozart's "Don Giovanni" as his character had some similarly unscrupulous traits to our shady Count Falletti.

RICHARD WAGNER - Composer
1813 - 1883

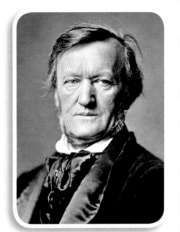

Richard Wagner is best known for dramatic musical compositions, such as the "Flight of the Valkyries," and the "Flying Dutchman." The piece that has enhanced many a wedding aisle is his sublime "Bridal Chorus."

Born in Germany in 1813, he grew up with his step-father Carl Geyer, whose love for the theatre rubbed off on young Richard.

As an adult, Richard's quick tongue and charming ways got him into plenty of skirmishes with the husbands of the many women with which he had affairs.

Another side of him, however, was not so lovable, as he was a staunch anti-Semitic whose political views ultimately got him vanquished from Munich.

Later in life, he and his wife Cosima, the step-daughter of Franz Liszt, were staying in Ca'Vendramin Calergi *(below, now a Casino)* in Venice. One evening, they were having quite the fiery arguement about one of his lovers, a young singer by the name of Carrie Pringle, when Richard suffered a massive heart attack and died.

Ca'Vendramin, a 16th-century palazzo, shares its walls with the Richard Wagner Museum and the Venice Casino `102`.

A plaque on the wall states that Richard Wagner died within these walls.

A
RICCARDO WAGNER
MORTO FRA QUESTE MURA
IL XIII FEBBRAIO MDCCCLXXXIII
VENEZIA

The NAPOLEON EFFECT
1808 - 1873

The Fall of the Venetian Republic

In an on-going effort to purchase military support from Austria, Napoleon promised to give Venice to them. Austria agreed. Now all Napoleon had to do was to conquer Venice.

This was a fairly simple thing to accomplish; because for over a hundred years, the Noble elite had enjoyed the position as the ruling class of Venice. Nobles were known to overspend on even the simplest of social gatherings and on reshaping the city to accommodate their personal sensitivities. Over time, Venice had adopted an anti-war mindset, and felt that their little serene island was their own secluded haven of peace.

When they found themselves in a cash-strapped position, it was difficult for them to cut back on their overly lavish lifestyle so they would continually pare down their military might until it was the size of a... pear.

After all, it had been more than a century since they actually needed it anyway.

Napoleon's secret sauce was that he was born with the ability to see the big picture, to see the end game long before anyone else did, and to quickly form strategies to get there before his opponents ever understood what was happening.

The all-seeing Napoleon was acutely aware of Venice's stance of all-peace-not-war and felt it would be simple to pick them off. Simple it was. In 1797 when he came careening out of the mountains on his impressive glittering mount, Venice had only 13 barely usable ships (down from 330) with a tiny cadre of Croatian mercenary troops left and was unable to protect herself. Additionally, Napoleon convinced the general non-elite population of Venice to turn on their own Nobles.

And so Venice fell, like a Palazzo of cards.

The Ping Pong Ball of the Adriatic
Napoleon took Venice and gave it to a pleased Austria. Napoleon had created decrees that aligned Venice with the rest of the Napoleon-owned Northern Italy, giving Austria a template from which to rule Venice.

A few short years later in 1805, France took Venice away from Austria during its own (ultimately unsuccessful) efforts to form the Napoleonic Kingdom of Italy.

When Napoleon was defeated in 1815, Austria took it back in an effort, granted by the Congress of Vienna that was working on many moves, to return peace to a Napoleonically-war-torn Europe.

For the coming fifty years, Austria ruled Venice, much to the chagrin of the Venetians who still saw themselves as the proud La Serenissima. In the 1860s after several unsuccessful skirmishes with Austria, Italy called upon their Prussian friends, who had recently defeated Austria. Prussia ushered Austria into making peace with France, partially by gifting Venice back to France.

Italy, at that time, was pulling together all of the straggling city states into a United Italy, and to show their support, France gave Venice to Italy to be included in the unification plan.

Today's Venice
This, my happy travelers, is how the Venice you know today became a part of the Italy you know today.

Epilog
Although Venice has since been transforming into a medieval tourist machine, the diminishing Venetian population still sees themselves as the mighty Venetian Republic, the Power of the Sea, La Serenissima.

Their Venetian language is now peppered with bits of the Austrian and French languages (and has since nearly been replaced by the Italian language), and their food has strong influences from both France and Austria.

As you are eating and drinking your way through Venice, don't be too hasty to assist in this transformation. Indulge in the remaining ancient wonders that are still the Great Venice: Funny spellings in street signs, great food, and the warm smiles of the locals.

The Golden Book of Nobles
A "NOBLE" in Venice means that you could trace your Venetian lineage back to a time before a constitutional change in 1297. A list of Nobles was kept in "The Golden Book" and was considered the only list of actual Noble families. There was no other way to be included in this book. (Except for the 127 families that paid 10,000 ducats each to be included in 1718.)

THE PEOPLE

GETTING HIGH

in VENICE

SAN MARCO BELL TOWER

The tallest tower in the city of Venice is the San Marco Bell Tower **64**, making it the ultra-best place in the city to 'get high' and take crazy amazing photos. The strategy: buy your ticket at the base of the tower in the morning when the ticket line is short. Don't go up the tower until mid-late afternoon. Reason? The sun. Earlier in the day, the downward view onto Saint Mark's Square will be largely shadowed. The best time of the day will be when the afternoon begins to turn golden, and the warm sun lights up the square below. Your long-range views will be the best as the days reaches toward sunset. If it is a clear-ish day, or one with spotty interesting clouds, you will be treated to one of the best views in all the world! Below are some examples of the views that you will enjoy from the top - and this is only the beginning. Don't worry, you won't have to climb, as the elevator will take you straight to the top.

Looking straight down over the Clock Tower and Saint Mark's Basilica.

A terrific view looking over the Doge's Palace, and the busy Venice Lagoon.

An unobstructed view of San Giorgio island lets you know how near it is.

The best view over Saint Mark's Square can only be seen from the top of the tower.

SAN MARCO CLOCK TOWER

Ships coming into the harbor can see this clock clearly from the water.

This complicated view of the Church can only be seen from the Clock tower.

Beware: If you are on the rooftop when the Moors ring the bell...!

A view down to the street below lets you spy on the tourists below.

The views from the Torre dell'Orologio - San Marco Clock Tower **66** - will be a surprise in so many ways. Procuring the tickets isn't the easiest method in the world, but well worth it. You will need to go into the lobby of the Museo Correr at the far end of the Square to buy your tickets and reserve your time slot for going up the tower. That appointment may or may not be the same day, so if you are in town for only one day, you may not be able to do this. Try anyway, you will be rewarded. They do this because there has to be a tour guide available to take you up. This means one small little group, and you. Nice! Learning about the clock is surprisingly fascinating, and the views that change at every level as you rise inside the tower are each revealing something new. One of my favorite photos of the city is top-right (above) as you can see how complicated the Basilica of San Marco truly is! And you can see this angle from nowhere else but from the top of the Clock Tower.

SAINT MARK'S BALCONY

GETTING HIGH

Up on the balcony of San Marco, this horse watches over the Campanile.

Although it isn't all that high when you climb up into Saint Mark's Basilica **53**, you are still treated to some incredibly unique photography angles. The day these photos were taken, a hot July summer storm was quickly passing through creating jaw-dropping drama between the horses, the sunset and that sensational sky.

Outside on the balcony, this horse watches over the clock tower.

The original 4 horses are kept in the attic of San Marco.

Climbing up inside San Marco **50** lends a feast for your eyes that you will never forget. The interior of the church, which is best appreciated from this angle, tells a Byzantine architectural story that is rich in technique, style, and heart. The gold gilting throughout, the stonework, the arches, the pillars, and the mosaics prove to the world the devoutness of the people of Venice.

CAFE MUSEO CORRER

This is a delightful little treat that goes unadvertised. Above the lobby of the Museo Correr **70** (the museum itself should not be missed) is a brilliant little cafe. During your hot afternoon of sightseeing, come here to this little cafe with high-backed tufted seating, cloth-covered tables, air conditioning, and a delightful little menu of goodies for all. The tables line the windows that look over the square and combined with a cool beverage and a light snack, you will re-energize and be ready to go back out to the streets to see more. Usually uncrowded, great tip!

GETTING HIGH

SAN GIORGIO BELL TOWER

The views from the top of the Church tower on the island of San Giorgio Maggiore are endless! In every single direction, you will treat your eyes to the largest array of vistas in in Venice. So many commercial and cinematic photos have been captured from this tower. And it's so easy to get to!

A bustling afternoon in St. Mark's Square can be seen clearly across the lagoon through a telephoto lens.

GETTING HIGH

The Bell Tower on the island of San ⬆ ⬆ *The picturesque Punta della Dogana*
Giorgio, as seen from the San Marco   *and the dome of Santa Maria della*
Campanile.   *Salute are seen clearly from San Giorgio.*

One quick Vaporetto stop across the lagoon from San Marco will drop you on the island of San Giorgio **174**. Once inside the church, an elevator will whisk you to the top where you will find some of the best views and panoramic photo ops in the entire city! Feast your eyes on the maze in the garden far below, then gaze across the lagoon at the magnificent angle of Punta della Dogana, the triangle-shaped end of Dorsoduro. If you get high nowhere else in Venice, you must at least go to the top of this tower. These are the ultimate best views of the entire city!

The back side of Giudecca island can only be seen from the top of San Giorgio.

HILTON® MOLINO STUCKY

From the lounge (below) on top of the Hilton® Molino Stucky on the island of Giudecca, you will get an unparalleled panoramic view of the City of Venice across the lagoon. On a clear day, you can see across the whole city to the islands behind it. Not to

BELL TOWER of TORCELLO

*If you aren't sure if you want to go to Torcello, this is the reason to do it: this view!
This is a completely different kind of view than you will get from any other
part of Venice. So get on that boat, and plan to enjoy lunch on the tiny island
of Torcello. You will enjoy a whole different side of Venice.*

be discounted is the incredible site of Giudecca itself (top left). Once called the Molino
Stucky, it was a flour mill that provided flour and pasta to the main island. After a fire
destroyed a large portion of the building, Hilton Hotel took it over in the mid 2000s.

FONDACO dei TEDESCHI

The Gothic building on the outside, with a big European-label shopping mall on the inside, Todeschi™ is a place to behold. If shopping for Gucci®, Feragamo®, and Prada® are your 'bag,' this is your destination. Three floors of elegant mall await your credit card. Take the red escalator to the top floor, then climb one more, and you will find yourself on the rooftop looking at one

LA SCALA del BOVOLO

Hidden somewhere in the middle of the San Marco Sestiere, lies this beautiful gem of a building. Exhibiting a little bit of Gothic architecture and a little bit of Renaissance architecture, this picturesque little beauty is an easy climb to the top of the tower. Once there, you will enjoy views all the way around! The tower doesn't seem to be tall, but remember that when you are in a city that is mostly a mere three stories high, a 4-story tower is all you need to get great photos from an unusual angle.

NOTE: the inset photo (left) of the Scala del Bovolo was taken with a long lens from the top of the Campanile (bell tower) in Saint Mark's Square.

of the best vistas the city will offer. You will look down upon the iconic Rialto Bridge, and you will be able to see the Grand Canal in both directions. The best time of day to visit for good photos is the early morning. Otherwise the dark shadows will hide one side of the canal or the other.

SPLENDID HOTEL

The little bar at the top of the Splendid Hotel is a little-known secret to tourists (unless of course, you happen to stay there). This is a great place to wind down the afternoon while treating yourself to a bird's eye view of Gondolas slipping through the canals directly below you. You will see eye-to-eye with the Campanile di Santa Croce degli Armeni next door. Your photos of the city will be from a unique angle. If your lens is good, you can get a great shot of the back of the golden angel on top of the Saint Mark's Campanile - all the way across town!

DISCOVERING

VENICE, A LA CARTE

DISCOVERING

There are only four ways to get through the city of Venice, and none of them involve wheels. Most are over water: by Vaporetto, by Gondola, by Water Taxi, or on Foot.

THE VAPORETTO

A Vaporetto is simply, a water bus. Besides walking, this is the main way to move throughout the city. The Vaporetti run every 10-20 minutes, depending on the time of day, the day of the week, and whether or not there is a festival happening in the city. You can purchase a ticket near the Rialto Bridge or at Piazzale Roma, then wait in the yellow sheltered 'bus stops' on the water.

THE WATER TAXI

The water taxis are easy to spot, as they are the fast and shiny classic wood boats that you will see all around the city. They can go into the smaller canals (the Vaporetti must stay in the main channels) and get you closer to your destination. The water taxis will also take you to the outer islands on your own schedule. They are quite expensive, but fast, swift, and a lot of fun!

GETTING AROUND on FOOT

Getting around on foot will prove to be the most challenging method of seeing the city. Venice is made up of 1,500 years of building, demolishing, adding on, tearing down, tunneling, bridging, and everything else. You see, Venice is made up of 118 islands, 170 canals, and over 400 foot-bridges. Add to that the crazy street names that change name every few hundred feet, and twist and turn straight into dead ends, and you may find yourself enjoying too many Spritzes just to get through it. But fear not: if you realize that every time you step outside, you will probably get lost, then settle with that, and have fun exploring places that you would have never seen otherwise. Here is a little guide to street names 20 .

GONDOLAS

Venice and Gondolas are an image that go hand-in-hand. Gondolas are as iconic to Venice as the Eiffel Tower is to Paris. Although currently they seem to be no more than a local tourist attraction, Gondolas have played an important role in Venetian history for 1,000 years.

Historically, Gondolas were a principal means of transportation throughout the canal-ridden city of Venice. During the 1500s, more than 10,000 Gondolas were counted in the lagoon, as opposed to the mere 400+ in the waters today.

For centuries, many Gondolas had an enclosed cabin ("felze") over the top to shelter the passengers from both inclement weather as well as prying eyes. However, today we see only open Gondolas. The cabins were outfitted with window blinds; **these were the original Venetian Blinds.**

Gondolieri

The Gondolier is easily identified as wearing either a blue & white or red & white striped shirt; a red scarf, black pants, and optionally, a white straw hat are all parts of the traditional uniform.

In the beginning, being a Gondolier was considered a low-class way to make a living. Because of their juxtaposition to private aristocratic conversations and 'situations,' it was later deemed that high-paid trustworthy men had to be hired. This led to a higher

The FORCOLA

The Forcola is the oar holder that is still hand-crafted from walnut, although cherry, pear, apple, and maple may be used as well. Each Forcola is designed specifically for its Gondolier to accommodate their height, standing position, and rowing style. There are 8 different possible maneuvres, including starting, stopping, forward, turning, slowing down, and reversing. There are only a few artisans who still create Forcolas today, but they lend a precise and detailed artisan's eye to their products.

The Ferro

Attached to the front of the Gondola is the heavy metal Ferro. It provides protection from scuffs to the beautiful wooden boat, and it acts as a counterweight to the Gondolier providing additional balance and control.

As with many things in Venice, the Ferro contains symbolism for the things that are most dear to the city.

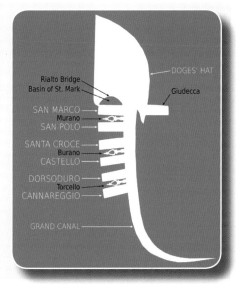

status for Gondolieri in general. Today, a good Gondolier makes upwards of $150,000 per annum.

To become a Gondolier, one must accumulate at least 400 hours over a 6-month period, as an apprentice to a professional Gondolier. Then, he or she must pass a stringent test proving that they understand the intricate maneuvrings required to move passengers through the narrow passageways. The Government doles out the licenses, and at the moment, there are slightly more than 400 licensed Gondolieri in service today; less than 5 are women.

• •

Tourists casually glide through the canals as the expert Gondolier maneuvres them through the labyrinth of city waterways.

DISCOVERING

DISCOVERING

GONDOLAS

These little boats have been adapted to perfectly suit the unique conditions of Venice. They are uniform in size and shape: 280 separate parts make up the 36-foot Gondola weighing nearly 1,500 lbs, taking more than 500 hours (3 months) to construct. All Gondolas are painted black.

Why is this Gondola bent?

The bent shape of the Gondola is not a figment of your imagination. They are all created with the left side larger than the right side by nearly 10 inches. This shape perfectly balances a single Gondolier with a single oar. A straight boat would require two people and two oars to operate.

Singing Gondoliers

Not all Gondolas will provide you with a singer - without an extra charge, that is. Nearby Gondoliers enjoy providing their passengers with entertainment, so they tend to follow closely behind or near the Gondola with a singer. Sharing is Caring!

1 & 2) A walk toward Zattare will lend you a glimpse of the Squero, a boat yard where Gondolas are constructed. They are made with real wood, and hand-crafted by professional artisans, just as they were centuries ago. 3) The beginnings of a Gondola require plenty of room for set-up. 4) There are many other rowing vessels seen around Venice. These are not to be confused with Gondolas which are only black. These colorful boats were each designed for specific types of races, games, and functions.

DISCOVERING

BUCINTORO

DISCOVERING

Historically, the Bucintoro was the Doge's boat, used to perform the nuptial ceremony of the marriage of the city of Venice to the Sea. Known as "Festa della Sensa," it is held annually on Ascension Day.

The name is sometimes given as Bucintaur giving it a mythological sense. In any case, there were four Bucintoro built: the first one was built in 1311 and the last one was destroyed in 1798, when Napoleon ordered its destruction after the fall of the Venetian Republic.

The last Bucintoro (pictured below) required a massive 168 rowers to propel it through the water. In addition, it took another 40 sailors to man it. The Doge's throne sat majestically at the stern. At 115 feet long and 26 feet high, it was a 2-story double-decker boat that could carry up to 90 passengers up on the second level.

"The Departure of Bucentaur for the Lido on Ascension Day"
Oil on Canvas by Francesco Guardi, c. 1775-1780.

This model of a classic Bucintoro is on display at the Navy Museum at the Arsenale **88**. It demonstrates the way the old Bucintoro looked complete with its gold gilting.

The Bucintoro used in today's festivals isn't quite as lavish as the old ones; the city is working to upgrade the Bucintoro to better match the original boats.

The Bucintoro used for today's Festa della Sensa is quite a bit smaller than the original, requiring a mere 18 rowers to propel it. Nevertheless, it still cuts an impressive image on the water.

ARCHITECTURE

DISCOVERING

The Venice you see today has undergone 1,500 years of learning, building, re-building, improving, and modernizing. The Venetians not only figured out how to survive on top of a bunch of mushy islands constantly surrounded by water, but they managed to make many of their structures last for century upon century!

From the Bottom, Up

As discussed 34, creating a city on soft wet marshy land was no easy task. After creating the man-made islands, the ancient designers went through a lot of trial-and-error to get the buildings right.

First, they tried what they already knew: using stone for strength, then nicer stones to create beautiful façades. Because after all, Rome was a great example of how using stone would last for centuries.

Using stone created a huge problem: the sheer weight of stone structures would sink down into the man-made islands and quickly become flooded with water. So they tried bricks, because after all, bricks are as sturdy as stone, they do not absorb water, and are much lighter in weight. Sadly, even though they could now create more structures that would last longer than before, alas, the accumulated weight of brick-based buildings would too soon find their way to the bottom of the lagoon.

What to do? Wood was not considered a good material to use for long-lasting buildings, and certainly not for buildings surrounded by water, so wood it would have to be.

Once they created a building with a wooden structure, they might cover it with a stone veneer to give it the ap-

Early Byzantine architecture was adapted using strong Western Roman styles as seen in this Torcello church.

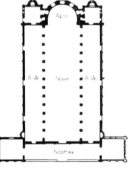

pearance of having been created with stone. Those fabulous ornately marble churches you see all around Venice today fit this description: wood on the inside, a thin stone veneer on the outside.

Medieval Beginnings

Many of the buildings and churches in Venice that were built before the Renaissance period (1400ce) were created using Byzantine rules of design that was borrowed from the Romans. A good example of an early Gothic church is on the island of Torcello, Santa Maria Assunta *(opp pg, bottom)*. Over the centuries, Venetian designers began to make changes to the strict Byzantine rules of style and created a style that became all their own which has been aptly labelled as the Venetian-Gothic style.

The Renaissance Movement

Architecturally speaking, the Renaissance movement didn't take a strong hold in Venice until after Jacopo Sansovino, who escaped to Venice after the Sack of Rome (1527), brought his architectural leanings with him. On his heels was Andrea Palladio from the Veneto area, who had spent time in Rome and learned how the revival of ancient Roman and Greek architecture had taken hold in Florence and Rome.

Sansovino and Palladio were the kingpins of the Renaissance building design in Venice, and along with several other notable designers such as Longhena, Bon, Codussi, and Sanmichelli, they managed to add a whole new dimension to the face of Venice. The flavor for Renaissance was ultimately replaced with the exquisite ornate tastes of the Baroque era.

Some designers were specialized, and helped to change the face of Venice: Antonio da Ponte, who won the contest to design the Rialto Bridge and Antonio Contini, the architect that designed the Bridge of Sighs.

BAROQUE ARCHITECTURE

Rossi's San Stae (left) and Longhena's Santa Maria della Salute (right) are splendiferous examples of ornate Baroque architecture in Venice.

DISCOVERING

CEILINGS

A common sight in Venice are the beamed ceilings. Whether you are in a private B&B, a hotel suite, or a beautiful church, the ceilings were used in buildings new and old. Wood is the primary material used for construction in Venice, and the beamed ceilings help to keep a building properly aligned on the ever-moving soft Venetian islands. The ceiling *(above)* inside the Scuola Dalamata is stunningly decorated in intricate detail.

CHIMNEYS

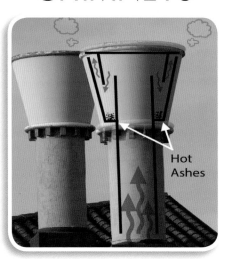

The odd-shaped chimneys in Venice lend a uniqueness to the sky-line. In the medieval times, roofs were covered with straw. A coni-cal-shaped chimney pot cooled the ashes before they could escape. The inside was designed with shafts that wind around giving the ashes a long path to cool before escaping.

In the image below, *"The Healing of a Mad Man,"* Vittore Carpaccio painted the Venetian chimneys as decorated with frescoes. *c. 1496, Tempera on canvas.*

Madonna del Orto (left) and Santa Maria Gloriosa dei Frari (right) retain their original Byzantine Gothic style.

The enchanting Ca'd'Oro (left) and the exquisite Hotel Danieli (right) are two sublime examples of Venetian-Gothic architectural style.

Palladio's il Redentore (left) and Sansovino's Loggeta (right) are a study in the sublime symmetry of the Renaissance architectural style.

DISCOVERING

BYZANTINE

VENETIAN-GOTHIC

RENAISSANCE

ANCIENT WATER WELLS

During the ancient times, Venetians were quite clever in so many ways. One of them was the way they collected water. Although they were surrounded by water, it was swampy, marshy, salty water. Residents still needed to find a way to get drinking water. The best way was to save the rain water as follows:

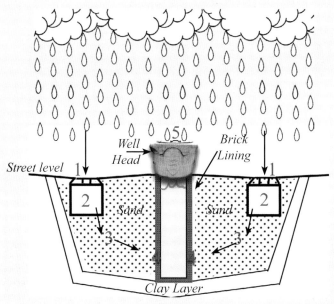

1. The rain water collects through grates at the street level.
2. The water gathers in tanks that release the water into the sand-filled cistern.
3. The water is filtered through the sand.
4. The water seeps through (more filtering) the brick liner of the well, filling it.
5. People lower buckets into the well head to bring up the clean water.

During times of draught, the key to the well head was entrusted to a priest who would dole out the water rations as directed by the city. Today the well heads merely lend one more unique item to the landscape of Venice. They are often used as the meeting place for a group gathering.

DISCOVERING

GARGOYLES

All throughout the city of Venice you will find representations of Gargoyles and angry lions, many of which are unexpectedly found on the outside of churches. These were not put there to frighten you; rather, they were put there to scare away spiritual demons, monsters, and disease.

GOBBA

The clever Venetians display their genius once again. These 'skirts' fill many corners between buildings all over the city. They may be made of bricks, or stone, or concrete. What are they for, you ask? They have two purposes: The Gobba *(hump)* or pissota keeps gentlemen from peeing in the corners(!). Additionally, they keep thieves from robbing people in the dark corners of the city. Do they work? You bet! Clever, these Venetians!

MAIL BOXES

There are several of these mailboxes hidden around the city. They were used in antiquity as a plea from the City to rat out your friends. Seriously. For example, the one on the left was to secretly report littering (or any sanitation abuse) in the Dorsoduro Sestiere. The one on the right was used to secretly report anyone who may be hiding their income. As the one who placed the note, your identity would be kept secret.

VIGILI DEL FUOCO
Fire Department

A water-based city has many challenges that you nor I would never consider. Emergency services has proven to be an on-going challenge in every city, let alone a floating city - where every structure in the city is made almost entirely from wood! Imagine having to respond to emergencies no matter the weather or water conditions. These men and women work hard to overcome these challenges and they humbly save lives every single day. Three Cheers for our Venetian fire fighters!

This mural covers the wall of the entrance to the fire station.

Fire fighting in Venice is much riskier than fighting fires on solid ground. These guys are heroes in the truest sense of the word. Daily they face the challenges of not only having to protect a city by water craft, but their whole city is made of wood. It is easy to think that fighting fires must be easy in a city surrounded by water, but this just isn't so. In fact, it is just the opposite.

When they respond to a fire emergency, they jump into the fireboat and take off, sirens screaming. If the winds are blowing, the water will be a rough, slow ride. When they arrive at the fire, their boat is bobbing up and down while they attempt to plug the hoses into the hydrants, making footing dire.

Looking out from the fire station garage: the fire boats are lined up and ready to go.

There is not always adequate ground space to place the ladders, nor space between the buildings to give the fire fighters enough distance to shoot the water. Often-times they must dangerously enter flaming buildings because there is no safer way to extinguish a fire or to rescue occupants.

Images courtesy of PIERLUIGI CULLOCA

The island of Giudecca holds many surprises. One of the more lavish is the Hilton Molino Stucky Hotel on the west end of the island, but it wasn't always this beautiful. Built in 1895 as a flour mill (pasta!), it attempted to compete until the 1950s when it finally closed. It left behind its decaying corpse, an eyesore on the beautiful Venetian skyline for the next fifty years. In 2003, it caught fire, in an extremely big way. Reports state that it was arson. Never-the-less, the local city fire fighters were handed one of the biggest challenges in their harrowing careers. The winds blew, and the waters tossed them around as they fought to extinguish the blaze. Of course, they persevered. Today, the resort hotel boasts being the largest hotel in the city, and the days of the eyesore are but memories of another era gone by, as it now presents its striking silhouette against the rosy Venetian sunsets.

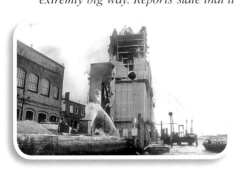

265

DISCOVERING

LEANING TOWERS

14 Luglio 1902 ore 9.52 ant.

Riprod. vietata   *prop.ᵃ ANTONIO DE PAOLI - VENEZIA*

On July 14, 1902, the famous Campanile of San Marco collapsed into a pile of debris. The prior day, a large crack was noticed in a Renaissance building that abutted the tower. Soon, according to locals, the bell began to ring by itself. It was learned that bricks and stones were coming loose from the top-inside of the tower, striking the bell on the way down. This gave people adequate warning to clear the area. After the tower fell, it left behind a massive mound of rubble. The only life that was lost was the caretaker's cat.

This tower today is now leaning, although not nearly as much as it was in 1902.

The image above is a re-enactment of the tower disaster of 1902.

DISCOVERING

There is something about leaning towers that captivates interest. Pisa is not the only city with a Leaning Tower, but it is certainly the most famous. Venice, unbeknown to most, has its lion's share of leaning towers. There are over 60 bell towers in Venice, and due to their antiquity, many of them are indeed leaning.

QUEST
Leaning Towers:

There are more than five, but can you find the 5 leaning towers that we found in Venice on these pages?

How many others can you find around the Venetian island?

Buttress
In this image, you can easily see the resultant efforts of the city engineers' attempts to buttress the back side of the bell tower of Santo Stefano.

LEANING TOWERS of Venice

San Giorgio dei Greci

Built in 1603, it is said that it had already begun to lean by the end of its construction. The church was created by Greek Orthodox refugees that fled their homes in Turkey due to the uprising of the Ottoman Empire. The tower has since been buttressed on numerous occasions. *See "Buttress" on the previous page.*

Chiesa di Santo Stefano

The Campanile (tower) was struck by lightning in 1585, melting the bells, and causing the tower to fall over the houses below. After rebuilding it, an earthquake in 1902 created instability, making it necessary to buttress the tower. This tower is still unstable today. The buttress can be seen from the canal side of the building.

DISCOVERING

DISCOVERING

San Pietro di Castello

This tower is considered to be one of the most unsteady towers in the city. The Church of San Pietro, although it doesn't contain much great art, contains the 13th century stone-cut throne which is believed to be that of Saint Peter. Until 1797, San Pietro was the most important church in the city. St. Mark's was not open to the public; it was the private church of the Doge.

Burano: St. Martin

The church was built in the 1500s, and the Campanile (tower) was designed by Andrea Tiroli in the early 1700s. Instability in the tower can be traced back to the time of its construction. The most recent repairs on the tower were completed in 1970. The tower is best viewed from the Terranova marble bridge in Burano.

DISCOVERING

FESTIVALS

It seems that Venice is one of the most festive cities in the world. It is. The watery environment makes it an ideal location to hold every type of festival under the sun. So they do. Here is a calendar of city-wide events to fit into your itinerary, because to celebrate with Venetians means that you are celebrating Life!

DISCOVERING

FEB

•CARNEVALE

APR

•FESTA di SAN MARCO
•FESTA della LIBERAZIONE

MAY

•PALIO delle REPUBBLIQUE MARINARE
•FESTA de SAN PIERO de CASTEO
•FESTA della SENSA

MAY-NOV

•BIENNALE - ART
•BIENNALE - ARCHITECTURE

JUN

•VOGALONGA
International Gondola Race

JUL

•FESTA del REDENTORE

SEP

•VENICE FILM FESTIVAL
•REGATA STORICA

NOV

•FESTA della MADONNA della SALUTE
•ALL SAINTS DAY
•FESTA dei MORTI
•FESTA dell'UNITÀ d'ITALIA
•SAN MARTINO

FESTA della SENSA

"Festival of the Ascension"

Held each year on Ascension day, it is a commemoration of two separate historical events: in May 1000 CE, the Venetians victoriously saved the Dalmatians from the Slavs, and in 1177 CE, a peace treaty was signed between the Papacy and the Imperials.

Today a flotilla of seemingly endless water vessels (mostly human-powered) led by the Mayor aboard his "Bucintoro" barge, begin their water parade in front of St. Mark's Square to the sounds of trumpets. They continue east along the island, then proceed across the

DISCOVERING

water as they head north toward the island of Lido and her Chiesa di San Nicolò. Once near the Church, the Cardinal blesses the Ring which the Mayor tosses into the water amid great cheering from both land and sea. This concludes the marriage of the City of Venice to the sea, an age-old tradition that grants the city one more year of safety from the waters.

Afterwards, a series of rowing competitions are held before returning back to the waters of St. Mark's Square.

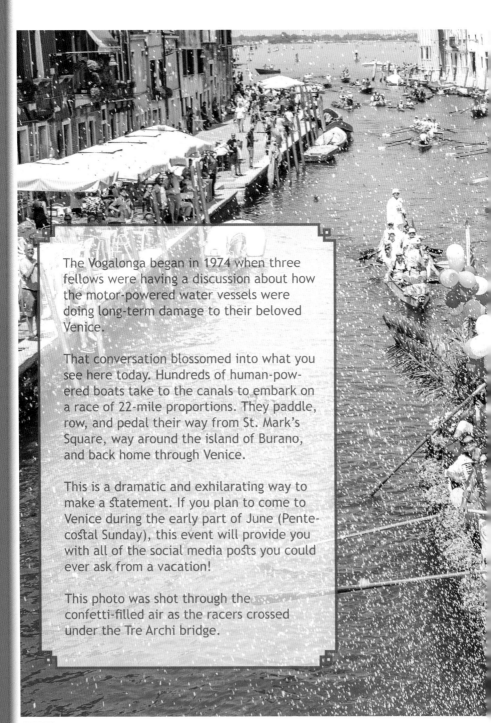

DISCOVERING

VENICE

LA VOGALONGA
Gondola Race

PATTY CIVALLERI

The Vogalonga began in 1974 when three fellows were having a discussion about how the motor-powered water vessels were doing long-term damage to their beloved Venice.

That conversation blossomed into what you see here today. Hundreds of human-powered boats take to the canals to embark on a race of 22-mile proportions. They paddle, row, and pedal their way from St. Mark's Square, way around the island of Burano, and back home through Venice.

This is a dramatic and exhilarating way to make a statement. If you plan to come to Venice during the early part of June (Pentecostal Sunday), this event will provide you with all of the social media posts you could ever ask from a vacation!

This photo was shot through the confetti-filled air as the racers crossed under the Tre Archi bridge.

CARNEVALE

Carnevale in Venice has enjoyed worldwide fame as the most sultry, masked affaire in the world of Carnivals. These images, courtesy of *Craig Barnes Photography (Los Angeles, California),* beautifully capture the dark mystery and intrigue created at the globally famous Carnevale.

Held annually, Carnevale occurs during the Christian period of Lent - the forty-six days preceding Easter.

Carnevale in Venice goes way back to the 1100s but was outlawed completely in the 1790s by the Emperor of Austria. Masks too were made illegal. However, in 1979, the Mayor decided to re-establish many Venetian traditions that had formerly been banned and used the Carnevale as the colorful focalpoint of this movement.

Today, more than three million visitors *(far right,bottom)* come to Venice each year to witness the most beautiful and festive festival in the world. Many go to unusual lengths to compete for the 'most beautiful mask' prize.

DISCOVERING

DISCOVERING

Carnevale Images ©Craig Barnes Photography, Los Angeles, Ca., USA

DISCOVERING

LA BIENNALE
Art & Architecture

Held for six months (May through November) during the odd-numbered years, one nickname for La Biennale is the 'Olympics of Art.'
It began in 1895, as a way for new artists to showcase their best works. It has evolved into a highly publicized international cultural affair, where every country can occupy a pavilion for their own chosen artists.

La Biennale takes place primarily in the Castello Sestiere within the Arsenale and its adjacent Giardini. In addition to art, it has grown to include Architecture, Music, Theatre, Cinema, and Dance. This growth necessitated the need to house exhibitor Pavilions all around the beautiful city of Venice.

If you are fortunate enough to be visiting Venice during this six-month period, you will find Pavilions in hotel, Palazzos, and exhibit halls all over the city for your artistic enjoyment.

These are but a tiny example of what you may find exhibited all about the city during the Art Biennale.

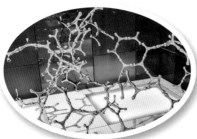

FESTA del REDENTORE

DISCOVERING

The year was 1576, and a beleaguered Venice had lost over 50,000 of its residents to the black plague. Doge Alviso I Mocenigo vowed to build a church in his honor if God would put an end to this dreaded disease in Venice. When the plague subsided, he kept his vow and commissioned Palladio and da Ponte to create il Redentore across the lagoon on the island of Giudecca which was consecrated in 1592.

Each year a temporary bridge is stretched across the lagoon from Zattere to il Redentore, and the Doge (now the Mayor) followed by a crowd of citizens will walk across the bridge and enjoy the Feast of the Most Holy Redeemer and give thanks to the ending of the Plague.

Later in the same evening, the fireworks begin. This is said to be the most festive stage in the world during this illuminated event. The amount of gratitude that Venice has for the ending of the plague is still evident today during this incredibly illuminated event.

This is the annual construction of the temporary bridge that runs from Zattere across the main channel to the il Redentore Church. The Doge (Mayor, today) can walk across during the Fesival to give thanks for ending the plague.

VENICE FILM FESTIVAL
Mostra del Cinema

DISCOVERING

Held during a ten-day period from the end of August to mid-September on Lido Island, the Venice Film Festival has been elevated to one of the most prestigious Film Festivals in the world. As a splendid showcase of the latest in cinematic trends, hits, and styles, it also covers a vast understanding of the history of the industry.

The aim of the Festival is to raise awareness and promote international cinema in all its forms as art, entertainment, and as an industry, in a spirit of freedom and dialogue.

The Venice Film Festival is hosted on Lido Isle, popular for its 5-mile long stretch of white sandy beaches.

REGATA STORICA

Human-powered boat races have occurred on Venice record since the 1100s, and probably long before that as well. The Venetian Republic had to keep a continual store of trained rowers on-hand because they were the engines that propelled the vast fleet of maritime ships under power. Man power, that is. A great way to keep rowers in good physical shape was to make an official sport of it: by holding rowing competitions on a regular basis and attaching a large amount of social prestige to performing well in those competitions. This attracted many a competitive male over the centuries to feed the constant military and commercial needs for expert oarsmen. The Regata Storica was born.

Today, the Regata Storica is held the first Sunday of September, and is popular for locals and visitors alike. People come from all over the world to compete in this high-value race, and to take home the coveted Red Pennant. Although no longer required for the military, the sport is more popular today than ever!

MESSAGES from our LOCALS

DISCOVERING

Welcome to Venice!

Exploring Venice means discovering the local culture as much as it means strolling around its squares and back streets. However, the high quantity of bars, restaurants, and shops can make it hard to distinguish the places where the locals go from the tourist traps, sadly, commonplace in Venice. We are an ancient city where, quality local businesses are struggling to survive, and many are replaced by low quality imported souvenir shops, or restaurants selling frozen food.

Well, we have good news! *We have come up with a simple way to help you have an authentic and fun experience in Venice while supporting the family businesses which deserve it!*

Just look out for our sticker *on the window or door of the bar, shops, and restaurants you come across in Venice. You can be sure that the place you are looking at has been carefully selected and has signed a charter with us to commit to a high degree of quality, sustainability, social responsibility and authenticity or innovation. Expect real Venetian food, authentic arts and crafts, or even quality fruits, vegetables, and cheeses.*

Oh, and if you get yourself the Venezia Autentica "Friends Pass" from our website, you'll be granted **a discount at each of the bars, shops, and restaurants** *as part of the program.*

Enough words, now! Have fun! We wish you an authentic and rewarding time in our beautiful city! A presto!

Valeria & Sebastian
Venezia Autentica, Co-founders

To buy your pass or discover more about Venezia Autentica, visit:
https://veneziaautentica.com/friends-hub/

Visiting Our Museums?

If you plan to visit the Best Museums in Venice, we have made it easy for you:

One Website, One Ticket, MANY Museums!

Visit http://www.VisitMuve.it to purchase your tickets.

DOGES' PALACE	CLOCK TOWER	NATURAL HISTORY MUSEUM
MOCENIGO PALACE	MUSEO CORRER	CA'REZZONICO
GLASS MUSEUM	LACE MUSEUM	FORTUNY PALACE
CA'PESARO	GOLDONI'S HOUSE	

Exquisite displays await inside the **Murano Glass Museum**

The mechanics behind the **Clock Tower of San Marco**

The sublime Veiled Woman inside **Ca'Rezzonico**

DISCOVERING

INDEX

PHOTO CREDITS

Our thanks and gratitude to all who contributed images for this book.

Cover: Keys – Pixabay; Grand Canal=PC; mask = Stock.adobe.com; map=©OpenStreetMap contributors; rialto=stock.adobe.com; Maps: ©OpenStreetMap contributors - https://www.openstreetmap.orgPages: Cover, 12, 26,27 Lock: pixabay, adapted by pc. Ice cream: pixabay, adapted by pc. Differences p 18: clipart=pixabay, open clip Patty Civalleri: pg 20, 21. Pg23 Fero=creativecommons. Pgs 24-25 Map:Nasa.gov Pg 28 sign=pixabay; Venezia Autentica logo. Pg 29: Misericordia=pc; dei Carmini=Wiki Commons; San Rocco=pc; San Marco=pc; San Teodoro=pc; Carita=pc; San Giovanni Evangelista=pc. Pg33: sunset gondolas=pc. Pg 37:4 horses=pc; Basilica exterior=pc; 4 men=Tiz. Pgs 38-39: Woodcut=commons.wikimedia.org Jacopo de'Barbari. Pgs 40-41: St Marks Square pano=pc. Pg 42: St Marks Sq=pc;. Pg 43: Basilica di San Marco: pixabay; DogesPal=pc; Bridge of sighs=Stock.adobe.com; Campanile=pc Pg 44: Clocktower=pc; Museo Correr=MUVE; Archeo=Muve; Fortuny=Muve. Pg 45: Musica=commons.wikimedia.org; Bovolo=pc;Grassi= wikimedia.org/wikipedia/commons; Accademia=pc. ¬Pg 46; Goldoni Th=wikimedia.org/wikipedia/commons; San Teodoro=pc; Fenice=wikimedia.org/wikipedia/commons. Pg 47: Music: pc; Santo Stef=pc; Rialto=pc; Tedeschi=pc. Pg 48-49: pc. Pg 50: St Marks night=pixabay; old san marco=commons.wikimedia.org. Pg 51: Tintoretto: commons.wikimedia.org; pillar=pc. Pg 52: 1,2,4=commons.wikimedia.org; 3=en.wikipedia.org. Pg 53: 4 horses, basilica exterior=pc; pala d'oro=commons.wikimedia.org. Pg 54: Basilica interior=pc. Pg 55: pala d'oro=commons.wikimedia.org. Pgs 56-57: Doges exterior=pc. Pg 58: Doges exterior=pc; Doges interior=pc. Pg 59: Bucintoro=pc. Pg 60: 1,2,3,4,5=pc. Pg 61: 1,2,3=pc. Pg 62: Sighs=Stock.adobe.com. Pg 63: Signs bricks=stock.adobe.com; bridge of faces=stock.adobe.com. Pg 64: Pano=pc. Pg 65: Campanile=pc. Pg 66: Clocktower=pc. Pg 68: 1,2,3,4,5,6=pc. Pg 69: 1,2,3,4=pc. Pg 70: 1,2=MUVE. Pg 71: 1,2=MUVE. Pg 72: 1,2=MUVE. Pg 73: musica apalazzo exterior=commons.wikimedia.org; interior= musicapalazzo.com; audience=commons.wikimedia.org. Pg 74: Bovolo=pc. Pg 75: Grassi exterior=pc; interior=Creative Commons. Pg 76: Goldoni top=en.wikipedia.org; bottom= unospitedivenezia.it. Pg 77: 1,2,3=pc Pg78: logo=pc; interior=Wikimedia. org; exterior=pc. Pg 79: 1,2,3=pc. Pg 80: Santo Stefano=Wikimedia.org. Pg 81: Santo Stefano exterior=pc. Pg 82: Rialto bridge=pc. Pg 83: Tedeschi= by Jean-Pierre Dalbéra; pano=pc. Pg 84: Skinny=pc. Pg 85: Arsenale=commons.wikimedia.org; Bucintoro=Wikimedia.org/commons; Giardini=Wikimedia.org/Wikipedia/commons; Garibaldi=Wikimedia.org/Wikipedia/commons. Pg 86: 1,2,3,4=pc. Pg 87: 1,2,3,4=pc. Pg 88: Arsenale=commons.wikimedia.org. Pg 89: Arsenale water=pixabay; Bucintoro= Wikimedia.org/commons. Pg90-91: 1,2,3,4=pc. Pg 92-93: 1,2,3,4,5=pc. Pg 94: red dining=pc; train st=en.wikipedia.org. Pg 95: 1,2,3=pc; Casino=commons.wikimedia.org. Pg 96: 1,2,4,5=pc; Miracoli= ©Didier Descouens. Pg 97: plaque, misericordia, grocery, no handrails=pc; Costituzione=Wikimedia.org ©Christoph Radtke; Scalzi=Wikimedia.org Marc Ryckaert (MJJR). Pg 98: skyview train-sta=commons.wikimedia.org; front=en.wikipedia.org ©Marc Ryckaert; quest=commons.wikimedia.org. Pg 99: 1,2,3=pc. Pg 100: Tre Archi=Wikimedia.org ©Unofeld781. Pg 101: Tre Archi & gargoyles=stock.adobe.com; pizza=pixabay. Pg 102: Casino=commons.wikimedia.org; toilet=pc. Pg 103: Tintoretto's house, Mori=pc. Pg 104: en.wikipedia.org Miracoli=©Didier Descouens; Dell Orto=©Didier Descouens. Pg 105: Jewish school= en.wikipedia.org ©Didier Descouens. Pg 106: sign, banco rosso=pc; map=openmap. 108: 1,2,3=pc. Pg 109: Misericordia=pc. Pg 110: Grocery 1& 2=pc; Costituzione=Wikimedia.org ©Christoph Radtke. Pg 111: Bridge, Tree, Playground, Park=pc. Pg 113: Rialto, erberia, san Giacomo, fish market=pc. Pg 114: St Aponal, San Polo; Goldoni, San Rocco=pc. Pg 115: Frari, Scuola=pc; Bru Zane=BruZane.com; da Vinci=Wikimedia.org ©Alma Pater. Pg 116: Erberia near, far=pc. Pg 117: San Giacomo, fountain=pc; quest=en.wikipedia.org ©G.dallorto. Pg 118: Camerlinghi=Wikimedia.org ©Sailko; man=beleefvenetie.nl; woman=dipoco.altervista.org. Pg 120: Mercato far, near=pc. Pg 121: San Polo interior=en. wikipedia.org ©Didier Descouens; Campo=pc. Pg 122: Carlo=commons.wikimedia.org ©Driante70; entry=pc. Pg 123: Stage, Lounging lady=pc. Pg 124: San Rocco=commons.wikimedia.org ©Didier Descouens. Pg 125: Resurrection=WGA.hu; Last Supper=WGA.hu; Crucifixion=pc. Pg 126: Pieta= commons.wikimedia.org ©Didier Descouens; titians tomb=pc; Donatello=commons.wikimedia.org ©Didier Descouens. Pg 127: 1,2,3,5=pc; San Giovanni=en. wikipedia.org | Public domain; dei Carmini=en.wikipedia.org | ©Didier Descouens. Pg 128: San Gio=pc; Vendremin= en.wikipedia.org | Public domain. Pg 129: da vinci=en.wikipedia.org | Pub domain; Vitruvian Man=Pub domain; 3,4=pc. Pg 130: Punta=pc. Pg 131: Bridge=en.wikipedia.org ©Didier Descouens; museum exterior=en. wikipedia.org ©Didier Descouens. Guggenheim=en.wikipedia.org; della salute=pc. Pg 132: Zattere=pc; Squero=pc; San Trovaso=pc; veiled lady=pc. Pg 133: Veggie boat, Fists, San Sebastiano=pc; Mendicoli=Tiziano Cini. Pg 134:

PATTY CIVALLERI

VENICE

DISCOVERING

Carmini=Wikimedia.org ©Didier Descouens; Margherita=123rf.com; San Pantalon=commons.wikimedia.org | Public domain. Pg 135: pretty canal=pc. Pg 136-137: big bridge, little bridge=pc. Pg 138: Accademia exterior=Wikimedia.org; Stealing=Wikimedia.org | Public Domain; Vitruvian Man=Pub domain; St John=en.wikipedia.org ©Didier Descouens. Pg 139: Slave=it.wikipedia.org ©Didier Descouens. Pg 140: Peggy=commons.wikimedia.org archives familiales. Pg 141: Gug mus=commons.wikimedia.org; Grave=commons.wikimedia.org ©High Contrast; Quest=pc. Pg 142: Floor=pc; altarpiece=pc. Pg 143: Salute exterior=pc. Pg 144-145: Punta della Dogana, wind vane=pc. Pg 146: Dining, walking=pc. Pg 147: Squero, San Trovaso=pc. Pg 148: Ca Rezzonico exterior, interior= MUVE. Pg 149: Ceiling, veiled woman=pc. Pg 150: Fists, foot=pc; Competition=commons.wikimedia.org | Public domain. Pg 151: San Sebast=en.wikipedia.org ©Didier Descouens; tied up=en.wikipedia.org; Coronation=en.wikipedia.org WGA. Pg 152: Mendicoli exterior=pc; archaeo=Tiziano Cini. Pg 153: Carmini exterior=Wikimedia.org ©Didier Descouens; interior= Wikimedia.org ©Didier Descouens. Pg 154: Campo blue sky=123rf.com; campo well=pc. Pg 155: San Pantalon=commons.wikimedia.org | Public domain; Campiello=pc. Pg 157: Pesaro=Wikimedia.org; Stae= en.wikipedia.org ©Didier Descouens. bones=pc; dell Orio=pc. Pg 158: San Simeone=commons.wikimedia.org; Mocenigo=pc; papadopoli= wikimedia.org ©Didier Descouens; Piazzale Roma= Wikimedia.org ©Didier Descouens; Costituzione=Wikimedia.org ©Christoph Radtke; Tronchetto=pc. Pg 159: Ca Pesaro=pc; Thinker=MUVE. Pg 160: San Stae exterior= en.wikipedia.org ©Didier Descouens; Torture=enwikipedia.org; Charity=WGA; Martyrdom=WGA. Pg 161: 1,2,3,4=pc. Pg 162: Dell Orio exterior=commons.wikimedia.org; interior=commons.wikimedia.org ©Didier Descouens; Ca Dario=pc. Pg 163: San Simeone=commons.wikimedia.org. Pg 164: Map=pc; spices=pc. Pg 165: Large interior=CaMocenigo; chandelier=pc; clothes=pc. Pg 166: Piazzale Roma= en.wikipedia.org ©Didier Descouens. Pg 167: Gondolier=pc; Tronchetto=pc. Pg 168: map=©OpenStreetMap contributors. Pg 169: Giudecca=pc; San Giorgio=pc; Lido=pc. Pg 170: Burano=pc; Torcello=pc; San Francesco=pc. Pg 172-173: 1,2,3,4=pc. Pg 174-175: San Giorgio top=pc; boats=pc; maze=pc. Pg 176-177: Yellow, beachfront=pc. Pg 178: map=Wikimedia.org/Wikipedia.org. Pg 179: Museum=MUVE; Basilica=Venicewiki.org; Campo=pc. Pg 180: Museum=MUVE; Well=MUVE. Pg 181: 1,2,3,4=MUVE. Pg 182: Bowl top=pc. Pg 183: Campo=pc. Pg 184: Egyptarchive.co.uk ©Jon Bodsworth. Pg 185: 1=commons.wikimedia.org; 2,3,5=Wikimedia.org. Pg 186-187: 1,2,3,4,5=pc. Pg 188: Lace collar=MUVE. Pg 189: Museum exterior=MUVE; Ladies=MUVE; Wedding dress=MUVE. Pg 190-191: 1,2,3,4,5=pc. Pg 192-193: San Francesco 1&2=pc. Pg 192-195: Gondola=pc. Pg 196: Polo=commons.wikimedia.org; Gentile=commons.wikimedia.org; Giovanni=Wikimedia public domain. Pg 197: Giorgione=en.wikipedia.org; Titian=en.wikipedia.org; Tintoretto=commons.wikimedia.org; Veronese=en.wikipedia.org. Pg 198: Shakespeare=commons.wikimedia.org ©Katie Jones; Vivaldi=commons.wikimedia.org; Tiepolo=commons.wikimedia.org; Goldoni=commons.wikimedia.org ©Driante70. Pg 199: Casanova=commons.wikimedia.org; Mozart=public domain; Wagner=Wikimedia Commons public domain; Peggy=commons.wikimedia.org archives familiales. Pg 200: Polo= salviatimosaics.blogspot.com. Pg 204: Polo=commons.wikimedia.org. Pg 205: map=©OpenStreetMap contributors. Pg 206: Gentile=commons.wikimedia.org; Sermon=commons.wikimedia.org public domain. Pg 207: Giovanni=Wikimedia public domain; Altarpiece= http://2.bp.blogspot.com. Pg 208: Pacioli=commons.wikimedia.org; hedron=ca.wikipedia.org; Vitruvian Man=Pub domain. Pg 209: Infographic=pc; Pacioli=commons.wikimedia.org Pg 210: Giorgione=en.wikipedia.org; 1,4=Wikimedia.org; 2,3=Wikipedia.org Pg 211: Tempest=en.wikipedia.org Pg 212: Titian=en.wikipedia.org Pg 213: Madonna=commons.wikimedia.org Pg 214: Ascension=pc Pg 215: Sacred=en.wikipedia.org Pg 216: Tintoretto=commons.wikimedia.org; Pg 217: Stealing=en.wikipedia.org public domain Pg 218: Tintoretto=commons.wikimedia.org; House=pc; Church=pc Pg 219: Foreshortening=pc; Scuola=pc Pg 220: Veronese=en.wikipedia.org; en.wikipedia.org ©Didier Descouens Pg 221: Last Supper=Wikipedia.org ©Oakenchips Pg 222: Shakespeare=commons.wikimedia.org ©Katie Jones; house=Wikimedia.org Pg 223: Mori=pc Pg 224: Vivaldi=commons.wikimedia.org; Pg 225: BG=stock.adobe.com; viol=pixabay Pg 226: Tiepolo=commons.wikimedia.org; Pg 227: Nativity, Triumph=WGA.hu; Banquet=ngv.vic.gov.au Pg 228: Casanova=commons.wikimedia.org Pg 230: Cell=pc; Overhead=pc Pg 232: Mozart=public domain Pg 233: Wagner=Wikimedia Commons public domain; Pg 234: Napoleon=commons.wikimedia.org ©The Yorck; Horse=commons.wikimedia.org public domain Pg 235-235: High=pc Pg 238: Bell Tower 1,2,3,4=pc; Pg 239: Clock Tower 1,2,3,4=pc Pg 240: Balcony 1,2,3,4=pc; Pg 241 Mark's=pc; Campanile=pc Pg 242: 1,2=pc Pg 243: 1,2,3=pc Pg 244-245: 1,2,3=pc Pg 246-247: 1,2,3,4=pc Pg 247-248: Gondola dinner=pc Pg 249: Vaporetto=pc; Taxi=pc Pg 250: Gondola bridge=pc Pg 253: Fero=pc; Gondola=pc Pg 254: 1,2=pc Pg 255: 1,2,3,4,5=pc Pg 256: Bucintoro=commons.wikimedia.org Pg 257: Bucintoro 1=Wikimedia.org; Bucintoro2=pc Pg 258: Church=thebyzantinelegacy.com/torcello via: WIX.com Pg 259: Baroque1=en.wikipedia.org; Baroque2=pc Pg 260: Mad Man=WGA.hu Pg 261: Orto=pc; Frari=pc; CaDoro=pc; Danielli=commons.wikimedia.org; Redintore=pc; Loggota=commons.wikimedia.org Pg 262: Well diagram=pc; well=pc; people=pc Pg 263: Gargoyle 1,2,3=pc; Mailboxes=pc Pg 264: Mural=pc; Fireboats=pc Pg 265: Fires=©Pierluigi Cuiloca Pg 266: New Campanile=pc; Old Campanile=commons.wikimedia.org Pg 267: Buttress=pc Pg 268: Leaning 1,2=pc Pg 269: Leaning 1=Wikimedia.org; Leaning2=pc Pg 270: Carnevale= ©Craig Barnes Photography, Los Angeles, Ca., USA; Bucintoro=pc Pg 270: Clipart=Pixabay Pg 272-273=Bucintoro=pc Pg 274-275: Vogalonga=pc Pg 276-277: Carnevale 1,2,3,4,5=©Craig Barnes Photography, Los Angeles, Ca., USA; Pg 278: Bienale=1,2,3,4,5,6=pc Pg 279: Redentore=pl.wikipedia.org ©Aisano Pg 280: Lido=pc Pg 280: Storica=Veneziaradiotv.it Pg 282: Logo=Venezia Autentica Pg 283: Glass Museum=MUVE; Clock wheel=pc; Veiled woman=pc Pg 288: thanks=Pixabay Back cover: Keys=Pixabay

Patty Civalleri is the award-winning author of a growing series of travel books for astute visitors to Italy. A wife and mom, she lives in Long Beach, California, USA, and travels to Italy as often as she can get away with it.

FROM THE AUTHOR

I present to you: The Keys to the City of Venice!

Like most people, I arrived in Venice and immediately proceeded to get lost. I found myself in Saint Mark's Square (doesn't everybody?) and couldn't understand why such a huge throng of people were just standing around staring. What were they all looking at?

As I wandered away from Saint Mark's Square, I noticed that the little streets were like rivers of people, all moving, all going somewhere.

I found the beautiful Rialto Bridge and noticed that crowds of people were standing on it, staring into the distance.

What I realized later is that tired vacationers find these two main areas in Venice, and don't know what else to do. So they simply look around for awhile, then leave.

Little did I know that as I walked through the little alleys and streets, I was passing hundreds of great things to do and see. The trouble is that in Venice, these great things are not well-marked. They are there, but kind of hidden.

This makes Venice somewhat impenetrable, with 1,500 years of cool things all around you. Unless you have the keys, you will pass them by, just like everyone else.

I wrote this book without taking space for restaurants or bars because you will pass plenty of those every 30 feet or so. You don't need a guide book for that. I wrote this book so that you can find all of those hidden "Easter Eggs" and discover all of the things that make Venice as special and as rare as a blue diamond.

Fall in love with Venice as I did, and come away with some of the most unique memories and experiences you will ever have.

Ciao!

Patty Civallen